'Frances is a true leader of our time. H[...] business leaders, entrepreneurs and tho[se wo]ndering what next.'
**Dame Therese Walsh, chief executive and independent director**

'A compelling read from start to finish. Frances's unique and fascinating insights provide inspiration and relevance to us all as we deal with the complexity of an ill-defined future.'
**Joan Withers, company director and chair**

'Frances's vulnerability and wisdom are enchanting to those of us who have often felt like business misfits. *Future You* is one of the most inspiring business books I've ever had the pleasure to read.'
**Anna Curzon, chief product officer at Xero**

'*Future You* takes the reader on a journey, one step at a time, along the road to innovation, curiosity and success.'
**Cassie Roma, creative strategist and co-host of**
**The Apprentice Aotearoa**

'Frances Valintine's leading-edge technology and insights, coupled with her pragmatic entrepreneurialism, will help you to think different about the potential of "future you".'
**Holly Ransom, disruption strategist, content creator,**
**and author of The Leading Edge**

# Future You

## FRANCES VALINTINE

### FOUNDER AND CEO OF THE MIND LAB

HarperCollins*Publishers*

**HarperCollins***Publishers*
Australia • Brazil • Canada • France • Germany • Holland • Hungary
India • Italy • Japan • Mexico • New Zealand • Poland • Spain • Sweden
Switzerland • United Kingdom • United States of America

First published in 2022
by HarperCollins*Publishers* (New Zealand) Limited
Unit D1, 63 Apollo Drive, Rosedale, Auckland 0632, New Zealand
harpercollins.co.nz

A catalogue record for this book is available from the National Library of New Zealand

ISBN 978 1 7755 4197 4 (pbk)
ISBN 978 1 7754 9228 3 (ebook)

Cover design by Andy Warren, HarperCollins Design Studio
Front cover image circular pattern by istockphoto.com
Typeset in Sabon LT Std by Kelli Lonergan
Author photograph by Lucas Jarvis
Printed and bound in Australia by McPherson's Printing Group

*For anyone who has ever picked themselves up, dusted themselves off and started at the beginning again*

# CONTENTS

**Introduction:** In the shadow of a mountain     1

**Chapter 1:**   Embracing change     15

**Chapter 2:**   The power of Gen Z     27

**Chapter 3:**   Taking the squiggly path     36

**Chapter 4:**   Finding freedom from technology     49

**Chapter 5:**   Chance encounters     64

**Chapter 6:**   The future is digital     75

**Chapter 7:**   Allies and adversaries     87

**Chapter 8:**   What makes a leader?     104

**Chapter 9:**   Starting a new chapter     116

**Chapter 10:** When life takes a U-turn     127

**Chapter 11:**   The future of work     138

**Chapter 12:** Confronting mortality     146

**Chapter 13:** Your online brand     159

**Chapter 14:** Sister wives     173

**Chapter 15:** Partner woes     189

**Chapter 16:** Imposter syndrome     199

**Chapter 17:** Power struggles     205

**Chapter 19:** Becoming an entrepreneur     215

**Conclusion:** Would've, could've, should've     223

# In the shadow of a mountain

## Life is a journey through time

When I was growing up, everything I knew and experienced was rooted in the ingrained norms of tradition. Each day followed a familiar schedule. I'd wake early, put on my dressing gown and gumboots, and head outside to feed the chickens and my pets. Depending on the season, there would be orphaned lambs or calves to bottle-feed. My siblings and I would set the table for breakfast, make our school lunches and pack our school bags. We'd then play rock-paper-scissors to see who would go out to the road to track down the daily newspaper that'd been thrown out the window of a passing rural-delivery driver's van. Our farm was remote, located 5 kilometres from the nearest town, which had a population of 8000. Everyone I knew had a similar life – our daily rituals had been shaped by generations of farming families who all knew each other.

By 1981, when I was ten, the BBC midday radio report in my small primary-school class was talking about global population growth, and the launch of Space Shuttle *Columbia*, which was in

1

turn igniting talks about the future of space travel. This period is memorable for coinciding with John Hinckley Jr's attempt to assassinate US President Ronald Reagan, and the extreme drought and famine that was unfolding in Africa. By the end of that year, the BBC news anchor was talking about what the future might hold. I wondered how these advances would affect the world I knew; I couldn't begin to imagine how the news stories I was hearing might affect me. It was as though dual worlds existed: there was my small community and there was the distant, unfamiliar place that other people lived.

While I didn't know it at the time, my world had many of the key elements of what we would now refer to as a 'circular economy'. Our community operated like a collective, where sharing and reusing was commonplace. All my neighbours and our family harvested food from the land, and everything that could be was reused, repaired or refurbished. My family had well-established cycles of activity tied to the months on the calendar, from food production to breeding cycles, to planting based on weather conditions.

There were so few instruments of change then – just the seasons. From the vantagepoint of our regular farming routines, I couldn't imagine how my rural community's strong traditions and practices would ever alter. I learned how to read a wind vane, a thermometer, a barometer and a rain gauge. For every change in atmospheric condition, we had a routine or process to activate. I learned to understand nature and its resilience through the extremes of weather. Living in the shadow of a mountain, I felt the cold of the harsh winter. Chilblains, from walking across ice-crisp frost-covered pastures, were a winter constant. Winter always felt so long as the cold set in, the only relief the fire in the lounge. I yearned for spring each year, impatiently waiting for the new season's growth to break through the frozen ground. Summer was the extreme opposite: I came alive as the long, hot summer days gave me freedom from school and a renewed sense of possibility. The start of the summer was marked by the arrival of university students, hired to help harvest crops. Summer meant holidays at the beach, sleeping under the awning attached to my grandparents' caravan. I would lie awake at night listening to the roar of the ocean as it crashed on the black sand beach.

In contrast to the other adults in my community, who followed the roles and aspirations of their parents, my father had an entrepreneurial streak. From a young age he began experimenting with different crops, looking for alternatives to his gruelling schedule as a sharemilker. By the time I finished primary school, our farm had been fully converted into a berry farm – strawberries, raspberries, boysenberries and gooseberries. These crops were the fruits of celebration, harvested as people planned for Christmas and New Year gatherings. I disliked gooseberries the most. Picking from the painfully sharp, thorny bushes required special gloves, and all for a fruit that was sour and bitter to taste. The advantage of this specific crop was that it was our only international export product. We were focused on getting gooseberries to market in the United States, as this meant better returns for our efforts.

Our family's livelihood was intrinsically linked to plants. If one crop failed, the economic repercussions for my family were significant. This risk meant we had to take extraordinary steps to protect the berries from weather conditions, including preventing frost damage in the winter months. On clear winter nights, we would walk down the aisles of berries, laying newspaper over the tender leaves. On extreme-frost days, a helicopter would fly low above the crop in the early hours of the morning, stirring up the air to prevent the frost from settling and to help melt the already-setting icy layer forming on the seedlings.

Being woken at 4 am by the sound of a helicopter flying metres from my house offered more than an exciting news item to share with my class: it meant a ride back to the helicopter base before the school day had even started. But, even as a child, I knew that having helicopters fly above our crops was expensive. Nothing else in our world could be defined in the same way. Expensive was a word that I associated with the wealthy families I saw on television. In my family, we always talked about value. Good value. We were like all the families in the area: our hardworking, family-operated enterprise made enough to cover the essentials of living. We sourced food from our vegetable garden, fruit from my grandparents' orchard, meat from the animals on the farm, and delicacies like kina or whitebait from the sea and rivers. We had a Hillman Hunter car that my dad bodged up by filling rust holes with fibreglass. I remember helping paint this car with house paint – it was two-toned, the top half a muddy khaki colour and the bottom half a mustard brown. It wasn't pretty, but no one I knew had a pretty car. The fancy cars belonged in the local car showroom or to the town's accountants.

It is only now that I look back on these times and truly appreciate that my parents were young, really young. When I headed off to school, they were just 26 and 28. The weight of responsibility they carried was significant by today's standards.

At home, I would overhear conversations about the economic reasoning behind their decision-making as they evaluated their financial priorities each month. What would have been a discussion about yields and returns on the export trading floor was simply a conversation about affordability within the constraints of a family budget.

Labour productivity is essential to every farming family. My siblings and I were allocated manual tasks from the earliest age. My sister and I knew how to have evening-meal vegetables peeled and cooked in the pot for the family dinner well before our parents came home. I recall standing on a small stool at a Formica bench alongside my sister, who, being two years older than me, could reach the kitchen taps.

The notion of value, and its relationship to revenue generated from the sale of products and services, was well understood by our entire family. From November to February my sister and I ran a small wooden roadside store, where customers would come to buy prepacked berries. Simple scales, a metal cashbox, and a pen and paper were all we needed to operate the business. In between customers, we would pack berries in the back of the store. In the busiest weeks, I loved working in this shed alongside the university students who were home for summer and working to make some extra cash. We had a small cassette and radio player that sat in the corner out back, on top of the fridge. We would all sing along, and in those moments of absolute joy I felt I could do anything. The students would talk excitedly about their antics at university. They spoke of experiences I couldn't imagine and people I didn't know. They shared stories of love found and love lost. They wore T-shirts featuring their favourite bands or funny slogans. Some conversations were hushed, as they censored parts they'd decided weren't appropriate for my consumption. Sometimes they would playfully put their hands over my ears, and I would wriggle to escape so that I could keep listening. My sister and I had autograph books, and we would pester these students to write sayings on the coloured pages. Sometimes I would lie in bed reading their comments and think about how clever they were, with their rhyming language and simple poems. Some of the messages contained words that I wasn't sure my parents would approve of, so I'd flip over those pages when sharing my book with adults.

In the confines of the store I learned the responsibility of greeting customers and processing cash transactions. As I grew older, I progressed from handling prepackaged berry punnets to calculating the amount to be paid by customers who had picked their own berries. Picking your own was a contentious topic for me. I would sometimes walk down to the strawberry fields, where

I'd watch as people feasted on handfuls of ripe strawberries, filling their bellies and just a few berries making it into the buckets. I was known to ask these customers, 'Should I weigh your bellies too?' The question was generally met with shrieks of laughter and the admission that perhaps a few berries had missed the bucket. I often wondered why these people felt it was OK to steal strawberries from us, especially as I knew that money was tight for our family. The pick-your-own offering seemed like a deeply flawed process to me, and I struggled to understand the economics of 'giving away' so much produce.

Even then I knew there was some kind of magic with trade. Goods in, goods out. Money in, money out. The key was to get the balance right so that the numbers on the right-hand side of the ledger were positive. There was never a time in our childhood days on the farm that my siblings and I didn't have a job. My parents are two of the hardest working people I know, and, as far as role models go, it's hard to ignore the significance of their work ethic in shaping my own.

When I was 14 I left the farm and my small town with my mother, sister and brother, and we moved to the big city. I left my old high school, filled with people I had grown up with, to study at a new high school that was five times bigger. Here, everything felt so fast, and much less connected. It was the first time I truly realised that not everyone operated by the weather and the seasons. In the city, the hustle was real; everyone was trying to get ahead and make the most of emerging opportunities. I discovered that people went shopping for fun, and there were jobs and careers in industries I struggled to comprehend.

I was fascinated by the different family lifestyles of my new friends. Some lived in big houses, their parents drove European cars, and during the holidays they would travel to Australia or even Europe. Most lived much bigger lives than me, right up until the stock-market crash in 1987, when their worlds collapsed. The big houses and cars vanished, the holidays stopped, and the conversation about the future changed. Disruption was real, and I saw the consequences of unexpected change as it played out in front of me.

My first real after-school job was working in the produce department of the local supermarket. It was the first time I had worked for someone who wasn't a member of my family or a colleague of my parents. It was also the first time I experienced the views of a self-confessed male chauvinist. My boss was a supermarket lifer who had grown up in the produce section. He took great delight in describing why women were less effective employees and why they didn't belong in his produce department. In his words, women weren't strong enough, resilient enough, or even very good at knowing the difference between varieties of fruit and vegetables. He made it very clear he was not thrilled that I was assigned to his team. I stayed long enough to prove that I was more than capable of meeting his high standards, but his negativity was all the catalyst I needed to seek a more rewarding job.

Job number two was a sole-charge position running the local video store. It was a brand-new business, and I was employee number one. The video store was one of the first in the entire region and I was so excited. Video players and recorders were the first consumer technology that everyone aspired to have. They represented the idea that entertainment could be personalised – you could record the shows you loved without having to schedule your week around when the programme aired. VHS recorders and players became the home technology of choice, as families saved up with the dream of watching movies from the privacy of their own homes. The technology was a monumental advancement in entertainment. No longer were we limited to three television channels playing a narrow line-up of national news, syndicated soap operas and sitcom reruns. Socialising round the television became a common occurrence, and binge-watching movies became a regular Sunday-afternoon activity. My friends and I would work our way through rented videos one after another in marathon movie sessions. We watched films from around the world and saw places, cities and cultures that we had never seen before. When I saw an advertisement for a job as a video store attendant, I was determined to make the role mine. My interview was held on a Saturday. I met the owner, and we talked about my work experience. He offered me a job on the spot.

Those early days of video-watching were the first time I contemplated how technology was changing the world. The war of global brands had started, and new technologies were promising new features, better quality and the chance to be at the cutting edge of progress. I learned about Betamax, the first tape-based technology, which was out-gunned by VHS before it ever reached mainstream dominance. With more and more people purchasing video players, the demand for rental videos went stratospheric. Video stores made significant money from rentals, but they also made good money off late fees. It was a familiar story – the collection of rented videos for the weekend's social gatherings was forgotten on Monday morning as people started another working week. Every day these videos were overdue, the late fees would increase. By the time another week had rolled round, the fees were generally higher than buying the videos outright. I was fascinated by this business model that relied on human laziness, and I marvelled at the ability to charge overdue fees, even though the customer couldn't derive any further benefit from a video they'd already viewed.

Customers would share highly convoluted stories and justifications for late returns. Most would elaborate in detail, trying to win me over with stories of sick family members or pets that had hidden video cases. These failed negotiations occurred night after night. In the end, everyone paid the penalty. Non-payment meant membership cancellation, and, as we were the only video rental shop in the area, it was our place or no place. One group of customers never debated late fees: people returning videos from the X-rated section of the store. They simply paid what was due without so much as looking me in the eye.

For 18 months, I worked as many hours at the video store as fitted around my school commitments, saving as much money as I could. My first investment was a Datsun Sunny car. Everything else went towards my goal of heading overseas as soon as possible. When I finally left New Zealand to head offshore, in 1988, I was still only seventeen – one year younger than the age required to rent the many R18 videos in the store.

I left New Zealand at a pivotal time in the world, when new tech-enabled products were becoming highly coveted assets of the wealthy. New technologies were changing the way we lived. I watched on as VHS tapes were challenged momentarily by the launch of the laserdisc, a large, circular disc similar to an LP record but played on a laserdisc player. They were valued for their high-definition visual quality and superior audio, but, as with the VHS, the laserdisc fell from popularity when the DVD entered the market. It was all over for the laserdisc by the end of 2000 – now it only lives on in an underground community of fans and aficionados.

All of my life I have been intrigued by disruption, and by industries that fail to innovate and fall out of market dominance. And no sector tells a better story of the impact of technology than the early days of personal entertainment. The quick version goes like this: DVD rentals dominated for a few years until they were replaced by low-cost DVD purchases. Rental DVD stores were replaced by direct-mail orders, which sparked the very earliest consumer courier-delivery services. Then, seemingly overnight, the dominance of DVD-rental chain stores plateaued as streaming media and set-top boxes enabled cable to be delivered into homes. Next came the onslaught of new streaming services, like YouTube, Netflix and Hulu. These big production houses now battle new entrants, including Amazon and Apple, who dominate multiple other industry sectors – and increasingly video and film too.

The story of entertainment over the past two decades is a story of mass adaptation and human adoption. Right now, as the world waits for the *Lord of Rings* television series, filmed here in New Zealand, record levels of investment are being spent. Amazon have stated that they believe their USD 465 million for the first series of *Lord of the Rings* will be worth every cent. Compare that amount with the budget for Peter Jackson's first *Lord of the Rings* film, at just USD 93 million. This transition, from one-off films to big-budget on-demand series, is yet again disrupting entertainment in our always-on and always-connected world.

I find progress and adaptation deeply fascinating, and this fascination has shaped my life and my career. Up close it may seem improbable that a girl from a farm who sold strawberries in a roadside shop would end up as a technologist, leading the conversation on human capability and the future. But if you take a 100-metre view of my life, the path becomes clearer. I see human potential as our greatest asset. I see knowledge and the ability to be open to ideas and learning as our most powerful tools. I see curiosity and risk-taking as our greatest enablers. I see progress as the catalyst that keeps us innovating and pushing the envelope of progress.

When people stand back and stay fixed in their thoughts, they become like a pond with no flowing water. Over time the pond stagnates. We all need a stream of inputs to stay current and connected, a constant flow of fresh ideas to support a healthy ecosystem. At 17, I decided that I never wanted to be stagnant, irrelevant or out of touch with the world I live in. I opened an Aladdin's cave of infinite possibility and let it wash in.

When we sit still for too long, the speed of change erodes our ability to confidently stay in the fold – and catching up becomes less and less achievable. The world is constantly evolving, and we must continually reimagine what we once thought to be true. Mass digitalisation of content, knowledge, music, stories and film will continue to change how future generations consume media. Nothing is finite or fixed. Who knows, one day someone may read this story through a device inserted in their brain that enables them to interface with technology using only thought. In reality, I can't even pretend this is a premonition – such technology is already patented and in trials. (Thanks, Elon.)

The quest to push the boundaries of computer processing, the human desire to discover and experiment, and new scientific understandings are all driving the aspirations and imminent realities of new technology. And each new technology has a corresponding human impact. We are increasingly adaptive creatures, and we must constantly develop new understandings and skills to stay relevant, connected and competitive in business and in the job market.

It can appear that technology is moving faster than our minds can keep up, but assuming this means underestimating our ability to learn. As a technologist, I recognise the value of not coasting. We need to stay relevant and informed, and we need to keep an expansive perspective on the world around us, but we must also understand the many principles underlying and informing progress and innovation, including economics, supply and demand, and motivation.

Understanding the concepts of value, trade and risk from an early age started me on a journey of discovery that has never stopped. I now work at the pointy end of technology and the development of people, as I focus on the future of work.

## Living is learning from our experiences and preparing for what comes next

I have been deeply immersed in technology and higher education since the late 1990s. When I look back at 17-year-old me living in London, actively sidestepping the higher-education system, it seems so unlikely that I would end up leading tertiary-education movements, pushing for relevance, flexibility and progress. When I first entered the world of higher education I was still in my twenties, and my students were too. By the time I was 40 I had transitioned from teaching undergraduates to teaching professionals and postgraduate students who were also my age. It is as though my students are growing up with me. This has given me an extraordinary level of insight into the behaviour of people over time, as they progress further in their careers. What I have learned is that age is a significant factor in how we feel about learning: with every birthday that passes, we put up more barriers. Our universities are filled with young people – the presence of a mature learner in a class is a notable exception to the rule.

I have to accept that, at some point, I will be older than my students and my relevance as an educator and advisor will be tested by people who will make assumptions based on my increasing age. I am prepared to be the oldest person in the room, but only if my knowledge holds up to contemporary scrutiny. Staying connected and continuing to be part of discussions is one of the most important aspects of being human – at all stages of life. Disappearing into the background and being excluded from the conversation is the scariest future I can imagine. If I fail to keep learning and understanding, it will be the first signal that I am self-imposing a limit on my participation in the world and disconnecting from parts of my community. I plan to do everything I can to prevent this from occurring.

My two current education institutes, The Mind Lab and Tech

Futures Lab, focus on the development of skills, knowledge and capabilities that will enable adults to navigate technological and societal change with confidence. Many of my graduate students are hoping to kickstart their own entrepreneurial dream, while others are just hoping to stay relevant and successful in the new digital economy. Over the years many of my students have been my inspiration – their many different careers and journeys have become part of my understanding. Many have shaped my learnings and my ability to see the similarities and differences we share. All of them learn part-time as professionals, at a time when most people are relishing the joy of being an expert based on studies they undertook decades before.

Throughout this book, I'll use the term 'adults' to refer to the group of people with established careers who study at my organisations. Most of them are aged between 35 and 55. They work in big cities and small towns, at large multinational corporations and small family-owned businesses. Each one has a unique life story, and many chapters have shaped their lives and careers. Very few have not had their career stalled or waylaid by relocations, family situations, bereavements, health concerns or the need for financial continuity. All carry self-doubt – they are concerned about their abilities, or worried about the difficulty of comprehending unfamiliar subjects that are, at times, intimidating. None have ever shared any regret for returning to learning. For most, their return to study as a mature student becomes a catalyst for them to undertake many other new activities.

Change is a constant, but grey matter is not. Our brains need stimulus, inputs and challenges to fire up and perform to the best of our abilities.

My adult students have shared thousands of hours' worth of their stories with me – their backgrounds, dreams, aspirations and fears. Over two decades working at the frontier of technological and people change, I have seen first-hand what makes some people live big, bold dreams while others watch on, wishing they could curate a different past or a more fulfilling future. I understand how decision-making and risk-taking influence our lives and achievements.

In the past 25 years, more than 20,000 students have walked through the doors of the institutes I have worked at or founded. Over 100,000 more have studied in one of my online programmes. Each one has dipped their toes into the unknown, seeking more from their life by exploring new information to plan for the future.

My life as a founder and entrepreneur, teacher, board member and advisor, has taught me that life is complex and simple. Harsh and beautiful. Long and short.

There is little that has happened so far in my life that I could have predicted or foreseen. Had I known where my choices would take me, I'm not sure I would have agreed to go along for the ride. But somehow, when the challenges have unfolded, as I've lived in the moment, I have found the reserves to dig in during the tough times and laugh through the good times.

Whether you are planning for a different career, developing a more impactful legacy or wanting to step with confidence into the future, you have it within you to create your own Future You. The first step is to identify how you react when faced with new or uncertain situations. Do you embrace change or deflect it? Are you open to new ideas, new people and new ways of thinking? Who do you want to be in five years? Ten years? Who is the person who will play with your grandchildren? Who is the person people will talk about when you are no longer defined by your career? Who is the person who will be remembered after you've gone?

Life brings many opportunities that masquerade as something else. When you stop making assumptions about what an event, experience or activity will be like, you may just find yourself stepping into a new jet stream where you discover the best decision of your life.

**CHAPTER 1**

# Embracing change

## Recalibrate risk and overcome fear

### Life isn't like bingo – and that's a good thing

In the late 1970s, when I was young, I spent a lot of time in the local community hall, in a room for evening classes and social gatherings. Back then local community halls were used for everything from Scout clubs to flower-arranging lessons. These community hubs have mostly been demolished now, replaced with offices or houses as populations grow and needs change. At this particular hall, I took disco classes in a small space my dance class shared with the local Women's Institute. We in the dance troupe proudly wore our homemade badges shaped like scallop shells with our names handwritten in purple pen accompanied by hand-drawn love hearts. Living in the moment, moving my hips to Donna Summer, I felt like a diva as I shared my self-choreographed disco moves with a very appreciative audience of women who watched on while knitting booties for the local maternity ward.

It was here in this hall that I first learned about bingo. It seemed like a very grown-up activity that involved bringing in tables from the back room and arranging hard wooden stacking chairs round them. The bingo caller's baritone voice would carry from the hall into the kitchen, where my friends and I would be sneaking arrowroot biscuits from the jar in the cupboard.

Bingo, I soon learned, was a chance-based matching game. It involved calling out random numbers that were printed on balls and matching them to the numbers on an allocated bingo card. There were big stakes on offer, so I was only allowed to play by sitting alongside an adult – the prizes of food hampers, sides of beef or crates of beer were deemed inappropriate for children. Each and every week the players would sit in the same seats with the same people, playing the same way, all while hoping for a change of luck to alter the outcome.

Over time, bingo came to feel like an anticlimactic way to spend an afternoon. I soon recognised there was no way to influence the game's outcome – it was dependent on luck. I soon grew bored of the monotony and joined the other children in the backyard of the hall, where we would kick around a soccer ball, skip rope and talk about who we knew with an Atari 2600 – the ultimate in personal entertainment at the time.

Even now, 40 years on, I think of those bingo cards, with their 25 small boxes containing a limited range of random numbers, and I wonder what the fascination with the game was. As a child, I put the attraction of bingo down to the chance to win a prize, but now I wonder if it was the attraction of weekly socialising, the ability to step away from routine tasks and share a common activity. To be honest, I am not so sure it was either. I have interacted with thousands of adult students, and I often see them operating as if life is a process similar to filling out a bingo card, as though the aim of living is to fill in as many predetermined goals as possible.

As adults, we leave behind the natural spontaneity of our childhoods to operate in predictable spaces and places that align with the actions of our peers, friends and colleagues. That 1970s bingo room could have been filled with people playing strategy games, developing skills and tactics to increase their odds of winning. But, instead, the participants were happy to try their luck on a game where critical decision-making was overridden by chance.

I wonder if the human fear of the unknown plays out even when we are in purely social settings – do we perhaps prefer not to be held accountable for our actions? Could it be that the attraction of a game such as bingo is not having to think? Is the fear of judgement, or not being understood, or being scrutinised, enough of a reason to stay in the safest lane?

Many people play a form of bingo with their lives. They let things unfold in a predictable and orderly fashion, matching each life event to a stamp-dated activity, just like completing a bingo card. There is an acceptance of inevitability and predictability as one phase of life crosses into another.

I have a soft spot for nonconformists and people who look at life directionally rather than specifically. These are the people who see life as having unlimited options, including the ability to form a highly personalised pathway that may lead to unpredictable places. While it might seem reasonable to assume everyone would prefer a full and varied life, very few people choose this road. The attractiveness of predictability is strong. Most adults prefer to eliminate risk and follow well-established norms – they don't deviate from the path to a place where certainty is less evident.

Why do so many people diligently fill out imaginary bingo cards, leaving so little space for change or spontaneity, or to reconsider where they're heading when confronted by new opportunities, or a chance to grow? It is easy to associate the acceptance of the status quo with contentment, but when you probe a little deeper you'll find most adults would've liked to pursue different careers, worked in other sectors or sought more personally fulfilling roles. What holds them firmly in place is their perception of risk – they find themselves unable to redirect their path away from the tried and tested.

## No growth without risk

Risk, or our perception of it, is a tangible thing that shapes our decision-making and our personal and professional lives. To create the lives we want for ourselves, we must first evaluate whether risks are real or perceived. And we must acknowledge that our minds are highly skilled at amplifying challenges.

Let me share an example of self-limiting behaviour I observed in a conversation last year. I was heading out for a walk when I saw my neighbour standing outside his house, hosing down his newly laid concrete driveway. I said hello and asked how things were going, and he responded by informing me he had lost his job six weeks earlier due to company restructuring.

'How are the job prospects looking?' I asked.

'Tough, really tough,' he replied. 'I don't have all the skills my sector now demands.'

I thought about this comment over the remainder of my walk, and when I arrived back home I decided to call my neighbour. I offered to help connect him with programmes that would build on his knowledge base.

That's when our conversation became interesting. He responded to my offer of help with an admission that he'd already declined a redundancy package offering him a training or development course of his choice. He told me he'd opted for help writing his resume instead, as he'd felt that would be more useful. 'I'm fifty-two years old,' he said. 'It's too late for me to reinvent myself. Besides, the technologies that're becoming mainstream in my sector aren't really my thing.'

I have thought about this interaction often since, wondering what he was so afraid of.

So much of our professional confidence is tied to our ability to do what we do well, and I can't help but reflect on the decision-making process that must've gone through my neighbour's mind. Did he realise that addressing his skills gap was a critical investment in his future? Did he decide to take on a less challenging role, knowing that there was a chance he would be less fulfilled? Mostly I wonder why a skilled and intelligent person would choose to limit their potential, even in the face of unemployment, when they could so easily gain the career development they needed with new knowledge and an openness to learning.

Businesses are only as good as the capabilities of their employees. If an organisation fails to invest in the ongoing development of its staff, the business will fail to recognise changing influences and customer needs. If individuals fail to pursue chances to grow, their skills gap will widen and their future prospects will diminish. To my mind, the least risky behaviour is to stay informed, to invest in your development and to understand current knowledge in your area. I recognise my assumption is flawed – if this theory were true, our institutes of higher learning would be overflowing with mature students. Reality says otherwise.

The combination of employees failing to evolve and develop over time, and recruitment processes that too often focus on very specific capabilities, stands out to me as profoundly flawed. Even with the right credentials, IQ testing and a cultural-fit evaluation, there is still a high chance a new employee will fail. Curiosity, inquisitiveness and creativity are overlooked in favour of hard skills, which are finite and self-limiting if not constantly developed.

Professional development is touted as one of the most valuable benefits of working for an organisation, yet so few companies invest more than a few hundred dollars per staff member in any given year. Contrast this investment with the large amounts of money businesses spend on insurance every year with no expectation the policy will ever be called upon. Why do learning and skills development receive such low investment from business leaders, when it is employees who determine a business's future growth potential?

You may have heard the saying 'What if I invest in my people and they leave?' countered with 'What if you don't and they stay?' The reality is, the real potential of a new employee comes in the weeks and years after the employment contract is signed. Compare a new employee to a smartphone: there should be a reasonable expectation that the person, like the phone, will improve over time thanks to new inputs and software upgrades. When you purchase a smartphone, you admire its apps and features the day you buy it, but your continued love for it comes from the features and apps that you add or improve. The value and importance of your phone increases over time, and the higher the perceived value, the stronger the relationship. Similarly, an open and forward-thinking employee who is an active learner and shows a willingness to develop is far more valuable to an organisation than a person who arrives preloaded with plenty of features but with no available upgrades.

We have all learned the benefits of firmware or software updates to our everyday technology – bugs in the code and the identification of new issues mean that our technology needs to be regularly upgraded to maximise the benefits. Not everyone has overlaid this logic with our own need to debug and run a new update every now and then.

Let's take an employee who has worked in the same organisation for five years. If you took a blank piece of paper and a pen and listed all the ideal skills, capabilities and attributes needed for their role, would the current employee still meet the criteria if their job was advertised today? Are they still fit for purpose in a world that requires constant adaptation to remain competitive and impactful?

Very few employees consider their value over time. Incremental knowledge and gains made on the job are often connected to pay rises or increases linked to annual inflation rates, but a person's real value is earned through a commitment to learning and discovery that extends far beyond tinkering at the edges.

Business risk and personal risk are much more closely aligned than they outwardly appear. We all have our own risk tolerance, operating like an internal gauge to determine how we receive news of unexpected changes or uncomfortable narratives. I have observed thousands of mature adults approach ongoing formal learning with the same level of anxiety that someone approaches a significant life-changing event, like the breakdown of a marriage or death.

Does anxiety about change explain our fascination with activities that have known outcomes? We stay in the same jobs, holiday in the same locations and shop in the same stores. We can be so hard-wired to pursue paths that are familiar that we miss chances to try things that don't have predictable outcomes.

## Overcoming your fears

Our world and the media we consume are overflowing with technological advancements that impact modern business. But, in most circles, understanding of these technologies is still limited to general themes, lacking the specificity or detail needed to actively grasp how it could benefit our lives and work. It is inevitable that all future careers in our always-on, constantly updating, technology-connected world will use and rely on data-rich, algorithm-based decision-making. It is our job to embrace this future with confidence and curiosity so that we can make decisions based on best practice, not out-of-date practice.

The problem is, we have a lot of fears that hold us back from realising this confident, curious self. Sometimes putting your head down and deflecting attention feels like the best thing to do. Most adults fear being caught out as someone who doesn't fully understand the implications or meanings of the headlines dominating the media. We constantly measure ourselves against rules and expectations that, in most cases, only exist in our own minds. The pressure of conformity is significant, and as a result we give ourselves very little tolerance to get things wrong.

From the time we are born, our network of friends and family reinforces and emphasises expectation. It might be strong career views held by parents, a pattern of decisions tied to educational advancement, or an assumption that talents will develop into a lifelong pursuit or vocation. I've had many one-to-one and group conversations with executives and emerging leaders who have shared their fear of making bad decisions, and the angst they feel as they confront their desire for change. In my experience, these views generally fall into five categories:

- **The fear of failure** – Some of us rationalise that it is better to remove potential risk by ignoring progress than allow for the slight chance of failure. This can include being unwilling to invest in new technologies or systems, or avoiding better, more responsive ways to do things. For many, the fear of the consequences that might come if they get it wrong is enough to justify continuing to fly under the radar. Lying low feels less risky than stepping forward to embrace change.

- **The fear of technology** – In today's world, all businesses and all professions demand a comprehensive knowledge of new technologies and digitally integrated processes. For some, in the absence of an ongoing commitment to learn new skills, it is easier to assume a fixed stance of defiance. However, deflecting the need to learn new skills, or relying on other team members to provide technical expertise, is one of the riskiest career moves you can make.

- **The fear of being vulnerable** – For many decades, being an expert has been a coveted position, the hallmark of a great leader. Command-and-control leadership is characterised by expert knowledge, strong opinions and the deflection of uncertainty with a show of strength. In today's high-functioning organisations, leadership is almost the exact opposite: leaders show a commitment to be open and self-reflective, and they own when they don't know the answer. Owning failure and mistakes doesn't always come naturally – many organisations judge human error in ways that are humiliating or penalising. These wounds can cut deep, and they can be hard to forget.

- **The fear of being stupid** – It has to be said: most people don't believe their years in high school or tertiary study showcased their academic potential. At best, most of us muddle through the formative years between 17 and 22, meaning our development years and learning happen to coincide with our most social and experimental selves. Jump forward from these days of youthful study to adulthood, and many harbour real fears that committing to study as an adult might reveal an intellectual deficit in the presence of professional peers.

- **The fear of a lower income** – We are taught from a young age that we are what we earn. Capitalism tells us to be financially successful above all else. We are taught to define ourselves by what we earn and not who we are or what we can achieve. Because of this, many believe that the only worthwhile career trajectory is up, and that their

salary will increase as their career unfolds. This is one of
the most challenging presumptions to combat. Aspiring
to the acquisition of assets and wealth has stifled
many great creatives, caregivers, academics and social
entrepreneurs, and prevented them from doing the very
thing that would make them happy.

The joy of ticking off predetermined numbers on a bingo card
may appear to be a sound strategy for living a rich life. But if your
future is dependent on the knowledge and skills you developed in
a pre-digital world, your life may end up much smaller and less
rewarding than you imagine.

## Taking charge of your future

Most life lessons don't arrive like a lightning bolt of absolute clarity.
They are slow-burning reflections that can only be observed well
after the fact. The truth is that there is no predetermined plan that
needs following, no box-ticking exercises that need completion.
You are the product of your own determination and curiosity.

Decision-making, like the ability to embrace change, is not a
skill we are born with. It takes experience and a willingness to
step into the unknown, knowing that there are no guarantees.
People are driven to change paths, walk round closed doors and
stand against the system for many reasons, but no reason is more
powerful than the motivation of personal experience or first-hand
knowledge. I have always been motivated by the desire to make
education relevant, accessible and meaningful. While most people
refer to me as a technologist, I see technology as a tool of progress
that can benefit many, the ultimate leveller – if only more people
had access to it and an understanding of what it can do.

Over the past two decades I have explored how people respond
to progress, and to unexpected situations that emerge without

warning. In the workplace, a new boss, a different technology system, an organisational restructure and unexpected redundancy can all be derailers. But they don't have to be. Change doesn't just happen. It is not an unexpected guest, turning up unannounced with a suitcase in hand. It is a process that is organic, fluid and responsive. How we choose to react to change defines how we feel, as change is merely an action and a signal of something new.

Many people I have worked with have openly shared their fear of the unknown. They talk with trepidation about new technologies, new business practices or changes in direction as though they are physical obstacles that've been planted as circuit breakers to interrupt the smooth comfort of routine.

Right now, the entire world is experiencing the most significant readjustment of the new millennium. We have all recreated our routines and adjusted our lives in response to Covid-19, and the need to stay safe has sparked high levels of innovation. Adversity has forced billions of people around the world to reimagine their livelihoods and to adopt new processes so their businesses survive. Since 2020, access to and uptake of online learning has soared, and education has been further democratised as people have jumped online to learn the new skills needed to navigate the road ahead.

There is no going back to a pre-Covid world. The global movement supporting mass digitisation, remote workforces and online learning is now deeply embedded in our everyday norms. Regardless of where you live, the world of business has leapfrogged into the future, and this is reflected in the adoption of new ways of working, the use of new technologies and the new work habits of people looking to grow and respond to opportunities in their careers.

No precast model or set of rules defines who you are, or who you should be. We all have the right to happiness and to pursue our interests and talents, conventional or unconventional. Whether you are just starting out on your career or you're in the shadow of retirement, the only thing stopping your mind from growing and your life from expanding is the inputs you choose to have. Step out from what you know, away from the autopilot world of what got you this far – it may just be the most enriching step you take into your next phase in life. But don't take my word. Test it. Open up the curtains tomorrow morning, look out to the world and be open to all the opportunities it throws at you.

# CHAPTER 2

# The power of Gen Z

Make way for the leaders of tomorrow

## Changing priorities

If you had told me how much the world would change between
the beginning of the new millennium and now, it would've been
well beyond my comprehension. Advances in computer-processing
power and new scientific knowledge have fuelled dramatic shifts
in our ability to develop and comprehend new possibilities. Mostly
I see our world being shaped by a generation who are only just
entering the workforce: Generation Z. They are young, globally
connected and digital, and they're standing up to call out the
errors of our past.

When I was young, it felt like all big advances were made by
people or companies with powerful authority. I never considered
the notion that someday in the future it would be possible for an
individual to drive progress or launch innovations that would
change the world. But I have since learned that almost every big
advancement – from the development of the internet, to space

travel, to medical breakthroughs – has generally come from one person with a big idea and the drive to change the status quo. But, before change can take flight, ideas need people who are adept at decision-making and committed to doing things differently, people who will look at how things are today and consciously and proactively decide to create a different way.

There are many early indicators of what our future will look like, and which technologies will become a core part of it. Already our reliance on data to better understand and predict everything from consumer behaviour to medical diagnostics is helping to solve some of the world's biggest challenges. But no one indicator of change is more compelling or visible than the changes driven by Gen Z, the world's largest population grouping.

If we are to truly understand change, and how our lives will alter over the next decade, we have to understand the influence and impact of the world's first truly digital generation. In many ways, Gen Z could be defined as Human 2.0, given the way they augment their world with the technologies they have grown up with. For them, the smartphone is an extension of the self. It is their primary source of knowledge, connection, commerce and entertainment. They are the first generation to blur the lines between the real world and the virtual world, and in the workplace they are bringing a different context that will inform the road ahead. They also have an understanding of where we are going long before most mature adults have even noticed the signs.

Gen Z makes up one third of the total global population. Their impact will overshadow the influence of past generations thanks to their staggeringly high numbers alone. In 2022, these young people are aged between nine and 25 years old. Tomorrow they will be our employers. They have never known the world pre-internet, pre-smartphones or pre-social media. Almost every service they use is online, subscription-based and delivered in real time. They are the first generation to watch the world in all its glory play out live, with no filters. Gen Z is exposed to more information, more data and more uncensored reality than any previous generation – they live in the moment, where there is no delay, no buffering, no waiting for the book to come out. Live events are transmitted directly into their lives. They curate their media feeds and observe life through real-time video. They see the world's inequality via live footage from the front lines, and they understand the benefits of technology and digitalisation on a level that no other generation ever has.

Gen Z will create and lead the businesses that will disrupt all remaining analogue fixtures and systems. They hold a common understanding of what technology can do and how they can deploy it in new ways to solve old problems. They understand the importance of personalisation, responsiveness and flexibility in ways that analogue businesses and conventionalists do not. We need to understand the impact this generation will have on our lives over the coming years. They will be the biggest change agents of the modern world, and their dominance and connectivity to each other will become a groundswell that busts through our ageing and irrelevant practices.

Too often in business we assume we will see change coming before it significantly impacts our world. We imagine our positions in the pecking order are dictated by seniority, and that we will continue to overrule the views of younger staff. This opinion doesn't only create blind spots for our future; it prevents us from understanding that younger generations are far more likely to be led from the edges than from the top.

When I was young, I was told a house, a car and a job for life were the ultimate destination and that these would all provide evidence of my hard work and success. How dated this mantra feels now. Today's youth are demonstrating very different consumer expectations. They think differently about lifestyle, ownership, even mobility. Many young people do not view a car, or even a licence to drive, as representing freedom. Instead, it's a burden of cost and unacceptable environmental impact. Their demand is driving the creation of alternative, more flexible options for personal mobility, such as shared vehicles, rental scooters and e-bikes that don't rely on public transport or private ownership. This shift in behaviour has led to the development of multiple new services in adjacent industries, including new forms of personal insurance for rideshare services, electric-recharging roles called 'juicers', and scooter and e-bike repair shops and commuter cafes. These changes shouldn't be overlooked – even in this single example of attitudinal difference, we can see the possibility of major implications for future road use and the way we plan our cities. I hope city planners are watching closely.

The social choices of Gen Z are less influenced by tradition too. They have a higher level of freedom in their personal decision-making about relationships. Like millennials before them, Gen Z are showing greater flexibility about whether to have children (or not), and they have less desire to follow in the footsteps of others. From the outside looking in, these younger team members can appear laissez-faire and unambitious, but nothing could be further from the truth. This generation makes decisions much more collaboratively, using the power of the larger collective to drive change and instil positive impact.

My neighbour, colleagues and business networks all have a huge amount of learning ahead to remain active members of the workforce. The technologies and scientific advancements shaping our future cannot be learned by osmosis or through passive on-the-job training. Data and automation define how businesses of the future will operate, and it's our job to learn and evolve with these changes, and to watch the actions and choices of new customers, including youth. This requires all of us to get comfortable with progress, change and doing things differently.

Our learning skills, which we first used as children, now need to be deployed again as adults.

The way we learn in 2022 and beyond may be different from how we learned in the past, but the reason we learn has not changed. Knowledge is our most effective defence against becoming irrelevant and it's how we prevent ourselves becoming relics of a different time and place.

## Big planet, big problems, big solutions

There are four generations in the current workforce, soon to be five. Each one comes with its own unique views, systems and experiences. However, we must acknowledge that our world today is unrecognisable compared to our world 22 years ago, when the clock ticked over to the year 2000. When I was in primary school, the global population reached 3.5 billion people. Our planet today supports a population of 7.8 billion, and it will continue to grow as today's youth reach childbearing age. It is expected that, around 2050, the world's population will stabilise somewhere between 9 to 10 billion people, due to increased lifestyle, relationship and fertility choices.

While we can assume some predicted trends and forecasts will play out, black swan events like Covid-19 are likely, meaning we'll also have to respond to unforeseen challenges. Nothing in the future will be a continuation of the past. We already face unprecedented challenges in food production, water security, housing demand and the needs of an expanding retired population who will require care, support and opportunities to be active members of our societies.

Gen Z are increasingly vocal about the world they are inheriting, and our need to act differently if they and their future children are to be able to live, work and thrive on this planet in one, ten and twenty years' time. They remind us that we, as adults, no longer get to make decisions that only suit our specific needs. We are all in this together, and our choices need to be ones we will be happy to share with our grandchildren and their grandchildren.

For many, the most significant risk we face in 2022 and the years to come is self-fabricated and self-imposed – it's the fear of the unknown once again. In contrast to our forebears, who faced many tangible physical risks and much shorter life expectancies, we have become overly fearful of imagined threats and unresponsive to real ones. The real risk in our future is an inability to foresee the consequences we'll face if we continue to trade on outdated assumptions and old operating systems that are well overdue for a reboot.

There is no better example of this than our delayed reaction to climate change. We have become ambivalent about its impacts, even as people across the planet experience extreme weather events as everyday occurrences. In the same way some use insurance to deflect business risk, I see people use insurance as a way to offset the risks of climate change. I am thankful Gen Z are holding court on this issue. Their voices are the most amplified and important. As adults, we must put aside our fear of risk and change and accept that we need to jolt ourselves into action – and we must let youth take the lead. For me, Gen Z is the gift the world needs to plan for the future. If we continue to operate as though we own this planet to the detriment of all others, our fate is truly predictable – and severe.

To kickstart work towards a different future, we must adopt unfamiliar knowledge, systems and ideas: consciously work through each component of our lives with a growth mindset and honestly identify what is really going on.

One method I use to do this is to sort known issues into three groups: simple, complicated or complex. Simple problems, in a work context, are problems such as covering key personnel when staff take holiday leave. A complicated problem could be a new commitment to better understand the culture of a specific team, or the dynamics that need to be addressed to build higher-level functionality or trust. Complex problems include challenges such as systemic talent shortages and the absence of key capabilities needed to move an organisation forward. Complex problems are becoming increasingly common to everyday operations, as business leaders recognise the immense levers of change that are forcing transformation in all sectors.

Many people only focus on the simple problems because they're most tangible, leaving the less visible, more complex challenges unresolved, like an unattended pot of water slowly simmering away in the background. When your mind has an unresolved issue brewing, it is hard to clear your head and focus on moving forward. If you resolve all issues – simple, complicated and complex – your mind will clear, creating space for new inputs.

Tinkering around the edges of change and filtering your problems to address only the easiest to solve just delays the inevitable. We no longer live in a white-picket-fence world – we are part of a highly complex, changing system, and we all need to be open to developing a better understanding of how to confidently move with the forces of change.

## Changing the game

There are many examples of businesses, across all sectors, that have failed to respond to changing market expectations. At the operational end of the spectrum, some businesses fail their customers by making them do more heavy lifting than necessary, such as a business that asks you to submit the same information multiple times instead of consolidating to one central database. Not only does this create high levels of customer or client frustration, it creates a high likelihood of data error. Riskier still is when businesses assume that products that've always had high levels of demand will continue to meet consumer needs. There are numerous case studies, and they have been the subject of thousands of MBA programmes – Blockbuster, Kodak, Nokia, Xerox, Yahoo, Tie Rack, Hummer and Borders. These businesses didn't read or respond to changing market expectations, and so failed to change their strategies at critical points in their development. Right now, entire sectors are facing the need to reinvent themselves to address sustainability, lower carbon emissions and different lifestyle choices, including access, conscious consumption, minimalism, veganism and flight shaming. The connectivity we all now take for granted is the ultimate system for amplifying and uniting consumers, and highlighting the failures of businesses that are unresponsive to change. Regardless of our individual roles, we all carry a responsibility to be cognisant of the signals of change and progress. Our livelihoods are almost always linked to market demands, and we must foresee and activate solutions to meet changing needs before new competitors do.

Gen Z are a living litmus test, highlighting redundant or outdated products and services. I do everything in my power to be privy to conversations among this group. Their ability to see opportunity and potential far exceeds the abilities of senior executives. Put a group of school leavers together and ask them to reimagine your business, and you will receive viewpoints and solutions that will blow your mind. Nine years ago, when I started The Mind Lab, we taught thousands of ten-year-olds who are now entering university. Even back in 2013 these students were outsmarting my team and using technology in ways we couldn't imagine. It doesn't surprise me that what I witnessed back then was just the beginning of their potential. They saw technology as a game changer in life and in business.

To make sure your youngest team members are active contributors to your strategic plans, you'll first need to discover and disband legacy or rigid systems. If you don't disestablish systems that prevent progress, it's likely to lead to factions, which will harden the resolve of the people who reside in the most inflexible part of your organisation. These people will meet new ideas with resistance to conceal their fear of the unknown and their inability to understand where they fit in the future of the organisation.

I was not born a risk taker or a systems thinker. I was happy following the rules of life and the changing seasons. I was an introverted, studious young girl who dreamed of working in design. But I soon discovered that life wasn't linear. The more experiences I had, the more people I met, and the more life presented me with opportunities to change direction. I now know that I was born with an intolerance for the systems that hold certain people back and unfairly push others forward. I never intended to get into technology or education. The reality is that these areas chose me. Once I was immersed in the world of learning and the development of people, I could see the many failings of the wash-and-repeat cycle of our outdated learning systems. As uncomfortable as it was, I committed to asking hard questions about relevance, access and control, and why some people were able to stay in their roles as gatekeepers of progress.

We all get the same number of hours in the day to do with what we wish. First, we should step into the shoes of the people we are preparing the future for. The Earth has been here for millions of years, and I hope it will continue to exist for millions more. But right now we are all facing challenges of our own doing. We have planet-wide issues to resolve, far beyond increasing dividends and shareholder returns. We may not yet be able to time travel, or talk to generations in the distant future, but we do have two living generations we should be looking out for: Gen Z and the younger Alpha Generation. They are relying on us to make good judgement calls. We know where we are today, and we all have views of the world we would like to leave behind once we're gone. Our job now is to be brave, informed and deliberate in the decisions we make.

# CHAPTER 3

# Taking the squiggly path
## Step off the conveyor belt

## Uncharted territory

No great insights come from working with data averages. The cluster of data captured in the mid grouping tells us far less than the data sitting at the margins. It is in marginal data that we learn to understand the behaviours of the outliers, the nonconformists, the dissatisfied. Stepping away from the grouping of averages, and away from the crowd operating in the mainstream, is also a great place to grow and develop.

As my career advanced, I found the courage to step out to the margins, to visit the spaces outside the norm. Today it is hard to imagine that I was painfully shy as a child. Among my siblings, I was the one who hid behind my mother's skirt and spent hours creating my own little world, happy and content in my own company. I observed the world with fascination, soaking in book after book, inspired by stories and characters.

It wasn't until I was around ten that I grasped that people

can create their own curiosities and follow different passions by pursuing their personal interests. I watched on as some friends pursued sporting ambitions, honing their skills in regional tournaments, while other friends took up musical instruments or danced their way through graded competitions. I dabbled in all these pursuits – netball, athletics, piano, violin and ballet. While I showed some promise, I knew I was never going to be as fast, graceful or musical as those around me. I even went through a stage of being a spelling-bee junkie. Spelling bees were a phenomenon that appeared seemingly overnight in my small town. We had a small pedestrian square, where a makeshift stage was established for the explicit purpose of spelling bees. It became ground zero for a fierce battle of words, as children of all ages took to the microphone to spell in front of the public. My hours of reading had paid off, and over time I developed the ability to see words in my head – a useful tool before spell-check and Google. Even now, decades later, I remember most of the words that stumped me – 'corroboration' was one, which now seems odd given its very predictable collection of vowels and consonants.

The first time I used corroborate in a sentence, I was trying to convince my mother that, at the age of 17, I was ready to head to the other side of the world without her by my side. I summoned up the courage to ask her and compiled a list of evidence that showed my independence and readiness to step into the world. To be fair, my list was short. But I was proud of it. I had money in the bank from part-time work, I was a pretty competent cook, I knew my way around a washing machine and a car engine, and I could navigate streets without a map (another valuable skill before GPS and Google Maps).

It's hard to describe why I had such an overwhelming desire to pack my bags and leave behind everything I knew, but the pull was immense. I had studied in Australia for four months in my final year of high school as part of an exchange programme, so the simple explanation is that I had the travel bug and wanted to see more of the world. The more honest response is that I didn't know what I wanted to do with my life, or which of my interests I should pursue. I decided that, with a little more perspective and some life experience, my 'calling' would hopefully emerge.

Looking back, leaving home at such a young age was a significant decision. It shaped almost every part of my future. If I hadn't boarded that flight to London back in 1988, I would never have ended up doing what I do. I would never have arrived in a city where I had to adopt new technology and be part of conversations about the future. I would never have developed the resilience to live in the moment, without fear of what comes next, and I might never have discovered my passion and curiosity for how people think, learn and respond.

My decision to abandon the idea of university or any other form of tertiary study was counter to the plans of my friends. All I knew was that there was a big world to discover, and I wanted to be part of it. Now, I find it hard to imagine the self-belief I must have had to jump on that plane to London. As my own children turned 17, I struggled to picture them leaving home for the other side of the world, even factoring in the improved connectivity and technologies from social media, smartphones and credit cards.

If you have ever arrived in a new country with only enough funds for a bed for a few days, you will know that the motivation to find a job, any job, is powerful. I may have been a little ahead of my time, but that first year in London I became a gig-economy worker. In today's world of portfolio careers, the gig economy has a certain charm to it – working flexibly across multiple roles and projects, choosing when and how you work. My gig-economy world sat on the other side of the ledger. I took every job I could, regardless of working conditions, to meet the hefty city rents and endless transportation costs. I found I could juggle multiple jobs if I was organised. I became an expert planner; my diary was filled with handwritten notes keeping track of where I had to be at any given time of the day or week.

It was here in London in 1989 that I first saw how technology was shaping the future of business and personal computing. I listened in on conversations as new software, including Microsoft Word and Excel, was discussed by the lawyers and bankers surrounding me on the Underground. London was awash with newspapers then, catering to every political leaning or level of intellectual fortitude. If you wanted the latest in the financial markets, celebrity sensationalism or unfolding global events, the papers delivered. Every day I picked up newspapers that'd been discarded on the train and immersed myself in the London that surrounded me, that I wasn't yet fully part of. The world was on the cusp of technological revolution, and I could feel it.

Just over a year later, in 1990, the concept of the internet, a vast computer network that would link all the computers of the world, was thrust into the limelight. Suddenly the idea that the big beige boxes sitting on office desks might one day be connected was more than a passing concept.

I was hooked.

Being in the right place at the right time is impactful on many levels. Think back to a time you first heard or experienced something that changed your life – the impact is still profound. For some, it might be the moment you ate the extraordinary meal that inspired you to become a chef. For others, it might be watching the Broadway production that sparked your love of working in the theatre. For me, it was watching the development of a new language based on technology. It was as though a secret world was emerging right in front of my eyes. It was new and uncharted, and it offered exciting ways to imagine the future. The little I already knew about computers and the impact that people claimed they would have was enough – I had to learn more.

Computers and technology were not my only passion at this time. I had discovered travel, and I was keen to learn all about places that I had only ever seen in atlases or encyclopedias. The world beckoned. There were entirely new lands, languages and cultures to explore. I saved every pound I could and, whenever my schedule allowed, I would jump on a plane and touch down in a new and exciting location.

Within a year of arriving in London, I had discovered charter flights, the small commercial airlines that would fill their planes with Brits heading off to warmer waters on holiday. For me, they were a new way to see the world. For less than 40 pounds I could travel as a waitlist passenger, buying last-minute empty seats and heading off to another new country with new languages and cultures to absorb. Travelling in the early 1990s was a much more lived experience – there was no internet, no cellphones, no digital cameras, no common currencies or tourist menus. I stayed in small private villas and guest houses straight out of my well-read travel books that rewarded my senses with wisteria-covered balconies, aromatic food and bustling, vibrant local ceremonies, music, dances and languages.

Every day travelling was a learning day. I filled my diary with notes on the people I met, the stories they shared and the challenges they faced. While drinking coffee was universal, I discovered that no two people or experiences were alike.

By mid-1990 I had left London and Turkey had become my home. I found my first full-time employment, working for a European fashion house that targeted the wealthy and elite with designer swimwear and beautifully styled jumpsuits. I thrived in my role, overseeing fashion shows and putting together catalogues that featured beautiful people lounging together in picturesque summer houses and quaint rustic settings.

My entrance into fashion was not as a design-school graduate, or through a network of established connections. It came off the back of the photography skills I had learned in high school and in my home darkroom, where I processed and printed my 35 mm film – this was a time when photography was still taken using SLR cameras and 35 mm Kodak film. Every photo I took needed to be perfect, as each image had to be developed and printed at significant cost before you knew if it was any good. My photographic portfolio was artistic, moody and creative.

To land my role I'd claimed I would save the business hundreds of dollars by taking better photographs and having fewer unusable images. For some reason they believed me and I got in at the ground floor. That was when the real work started. I turned up to every event I could. I got busy helping others and I worked in areas well outside my comfort zone, assisting designers and event planners with the things that made their jobs easier. If they needed a runner, I was their girl. If they needed coffee, I was always on call. If they needed to practise their English, I would sit and patiently work alongside them and assist with their comprehension. It was a huge learning experience for me. I came to realise I was more capable than I had given myself credit for – I was happy putting my hand up even when I had no idea what I was committing to.

In the summer months I moved from Istanbul to the town of Bodrum, where the summer crowds from around Europe poured into the local resorts in their thousands. My life was far removed from the tour-package, piña colada-fuelled existence of the tourist community who stayed poolside at their resorts. I worked with some of the local heavy hitters in fashion, and they lived luxurious lifestyles, taking jet boats out under the cover of darkness to private nightclubs and heavily guarded events. My Turkey was culturally rich, filled with artists and creatives and people driving for change and progress as the cities increasingly reflected mainstream European culture and the uprising of a new generation of leaders.

Time passed by and the seasons changed, and soon another significant shift was unfolding. I watched as the number of fashion shows began to diminish and tourist numbers decreased, until eventually the tourists disappeared completely. By the end of 1990, I was advised that, as a foreign national, I was required to leave the country. The Gulf War was intensifying, and the United States was flying missions into the Middle East war zone from Turkish military bases. All non-essential foreign workers were ordered to leave the country. My options were limited. With no other plan, I headed back home to New Zealand.

## The path less trodden is the path most scrutinised

This was when my life entered an unexpected new phase. I had international experience and a range of new skills, and I was fiercely independent, capable and motivated, but, at only 20 years old, I was an anomaly. My peers and friends still hadn't graduated from university. Travelling and living in different countries had been life-changing for me, but my assumption that I would easily fit back in at home was far from my reality. My world had changed and I had changed, but my experiences from my time abroad created unexpected challenges for potential employers, who struggled to put my knowledge and skills into a definable box. This was a time when men held the majority of influence and authority in the workplace, and they were often dismissive of my overseas experience and critical of my decision to head offshore so young. They showed no recognition that independence and resilience were valuable traits that would benefit an employer, and when I tried to stress this my words fell on deaf ears.

It was one closed door after another. I soon grew frustrated with the lack of imagination shown by some of the employers I met. They all had a predefined view of what they were looking for, and I realised what they were looking for wasn't me.

This got me thinking about the prescriptive boxes we put round people, careers and timeframes. Imagine if we could all reverse-engineer our lives. What if we started from our deathbeds and worked backwards? What if we knew how many years we had ahead with great certainty? Would we choose to work differently or respond to life with more intention? Would we choose to work for organisations that are better aligned with our values? Would we spend more time with our loved ones building connections? Would we take more risks and pass judgement less often? I am certain we would spend significantly less time listening to what others think we should be doing.

My first overseas experience was the beginning of a lifetime of travel and exploration. Each journey has taught me more about people, humanity and business than any book could. By stepping off the conveyor belt of normal practice to become a citizen of the world, I had also become a nonconformist and employers didn't know where I fitted. My return to New Zealand was met with many unsolicited opinions about what I should be doing, or what I would need to do to get back on track.

*Back on track?* I was constantly bewildered by this mysterious track that I should have been following. What was so important that I should miss the opportunity to live and work overseas, and why did everyone have an opinion about what I should be doing?

It turns out that the path less trodden is also the path most scrutinised. Nobody blinks an eye if you step into a university degree straight after high school, but any deviation from this path is apparently fair game for in-depth lines of questioning. The more years that pass, the more intense the scrutiny becomes. *What do you mean you're quitting law? Why would you leave such a great company?* Or my favourite: *Why on earth would you go back to study? Aren't you a little old for that?*

Ageism is a well-known issue for people in the later years of their career, but I discovered first-hand that youth face a different form of bias. Maturity covers such a broad spectrum of actions. Even today I see highly motivated young people who are still in school starting their own businesses, while some university graduates have never worked a day in their life. For me, the ability to be a self-starter is a strength at any age.

I dream of the day that media headlines celebrate people who deviate from predetermined paths. When an adult pursues a long-held dream to develop new skills, or steps back from the stresses of what they are doing, they must fight an internal battle about making a 'selfish' decision. Sticking to what you know, being the breadwinner and aiming for the top has become the mantra of the developed world.

Do we overestimate and assume that things will get better if only we get that promotion, or the better house, or the better title? Are we so conditioned to the way our lives play out that we can't comprehend how things might look if we take a lesser-known path?

## A sudden moment of clarity

Ask anyone who has beaten a major illness or survived a serious accident: one of the most powerful catalysts for behavioural change is the threat of death. There's nothing quite like a near-death or life-threatening experience. Life is full of an abundance of options, and when those choices are suddenly removed by an unexpected, life-threatening reality, extreme clarity will often emerge.

I know exactly when that clarity came for me. I was flying to Auckland with two friends in a single-engine Cessna after a long-weekend getaway in Napier. It was Labour Day 1995 and the sun was shining on the sea below us. One of my friends was the pilot, the other was the navigator. We were flying in tandem with another small plane, which carried another group of friends who were also flying back to Auckland. As we headed home, we ducked and dived side by side through fluffy white clouds. Soon, our friends' plane dipped out to land at the aerodrome in Ardmore in South Auckland, while we carried on to Whenuapai airport in the north. We never made it.

Flying low above the North Shore beaches, we laughed and admired the boats on the water and the early-season swimmers enjoying a brisk October dip. As we soared high above Auckland city, over the East Coast Bays, the plane chugged and then stalled. I watched in slow motion as the propeller transitioned from a blur of powered energy to two distinct blades frozen motionless and silent. I looked out the window to the ocean beneath us as the Mayday call was made. We had no power, and we were falling fast. The Mayday responder crackled back through the speaker: 'We can't hear you. You're breaking up.' Even today it seems like a wholly inappropriate message to share with the pilot and passengers of a plane that's in free fall.

Sitting behind the pilot and navigator, as the plane was freefalling from the sky to the ocean below, I calmly picked up a leather jacket from the seat next to me and put it on back to front so that the back of the jacket was across my chest. I picked up my large early-edition cellphone and my SLR camera and tucked them into the jacket so that they wouldn't fly forward on impact. I could see large protruding cliffs ahead. We were heading directly towards them.

Without any power to lift the plane, the pilot pulled hard on the steering yoke to aim for a gap in the cliffs that was about the same width as the wingspan of the plane. I knew we were on a collision course and our chance of survival was low. As long, drawn-out seconds of complete terror played out in my mind, I folded my body over on my seat to adopt the brace position that I had seen demonstrated so many times before on commercial flights. I waited for impact. No one said a word. My eyes were closed and my mind was filled with thoughts of my loved ones. The moment froze in time.

I waited, but the impact with the cliffs didn't come. The pilot held hard on to the yoke, desperately willing the plane to lift, and miraculously he managed to pull it through the gap in the cliffs so that we skimmed across the boulders protruding from the clifftop and hit the beach. Hard.

The minutes after the crash are a blur. We had all survived and we climbed out of the plane to the wails of ambulances and fire engines. I laughed hysterically. Maybe we all did. I honestly don't recall.

The first moment my family knew what had happened was when they watched the evening news. The next day both my plane companions proposed to their girlfriends. I made a commitment to myself never to take life for granted. Every day was a chance to learn, to share, to teach and to laugh. I still live by these values.

We all face unexpected challenges and unforeseen tragedy and sadness. Each morning we wake with the reasonable expectation that the day will pass somewhat predictably and, before we know it, we're back in front of the bathroom mirror brushing our teeth before bed. But we all know not every day pans out this way. Some days come crashing down around us. One phone call, one conversation, one experience can alter our paths and create an entirely different future.

What we do in the days, weeks and months following adversity is one of the most significant, yet unplanned, learning experiences of our lives. There is no rule book that can tell you how you should behave or respond, or what your next step should be. What I do know is that, when life pulls every security out from under your feet, you need to find a way to work through it.

Adversity has a way of highlighting what's really important. The more life throws at us, the more we see a way forward. When an unexpected traumatic event rolls in it can feel like an inescapable blow, but over time a new level of resilience will emerge. That resilience might feel rugged and uninformed, and sometimes it's so unfamiliar it can feel like it belongs to someone else, but one certainty in life is that we are all dealt life-changing adversity. In these moments I find strength in the knowledge that, in time, this period will pass.

We all evolve, adapt, learn and respond differently to crises. Some people are quick to see the patterns of disruption coming; others don't see the changing of the guard until it's too late. Some people prefer to simply put their heads down and let life pass overhead, hoping it won't reach in and capture them unaware.

## Your path is what you make it

Living life within the range of averages comes with less risk, greater acceptance and far greater reinforcement from popular decision-making. But it also comes with an absence of knowledge about what you could've otherwise achieved, or what great heights you could've reached, if only you'd taken one step beyond what you already knew.

If you want to make a difference, change outcomes or start a movement, you must find the courage to stand apart. Leading from the edge provides a platform for progress and a stage for change. The world is evolving around us at a speed that is hard to comprehend. The qualities a leader needs today are very different from the characteristics of the leaders of the past. We need highly informed, visionary business supporters who can lead us along the road less travelled. We need people who can step out in front to encourage others on the journey.

It is hard to step away from the comfort of averages, but the rewards are abundant. Too many people would rather stay on familiar terrain, and I have learned that there is little that can be done to sway the views or decisions of those who choose not to be open to new ideas. But, if you are willing to stand up for what you believe in, move out to the fringes. Here, you will have every opportunity to freely share your own narrative and to find kindred spirits. Progress takes just one person with a brave heart and the desire to create a different type of legacy.

Some of the biggest changes I made in the first decades of my life were in many ways immature in their thought and planning. But these decisions helped me develop some of the most beneficial tools of my life – resilience, independence, financial literacy and cultural competency. Moving to new countries and immersing myself in different environments forced me to become comfortable with rapid decision-making responsibilities at a young age, and it taught me to back my own judgement. I am grateful that my family was supportive of my desire to head offshore – in the modern world, we can be overly protective of our children and insist on making their decisions for them.

I wonder whether those early days of being exposed to technology on the trains in London planted the seed for my future, whether somewhere in my subconscious I created an alternative neural pathway that enabled a dual system of where my future would go. Most doors open because you just happen to be at the right place at the right time, but I also believe that you're in the right place because you're meant to be there. Closed doors are barriers to be walked around, as well as catalysts of greater progress.

I'm still trying to figure out why I would've been significantly challenged if my own children had asked to fly to London at 17. What if, by trying to protect ourselves and our children, we are removing their chance to discover who they really are, and what they're capable of?

It didn't take a plane crash for me to know life was for living, but it certainly added perspective. It would be helpful if life came with clearer instructions about the lessons we learn as new situations unfold, but in the absence of this I'm happy to roll the dice and see where it takes me.

## CHAPTER 4

# Finding freedom from technology

## Take time to reset and reflect

### A trip to Yap

It's the mid-2000s and my sister-in-law and I are travelling to Yap, a tiny island located in the Federated States of Micronesia. To reach Yap we have to overnight on the island of Guam, a US military stronghold that is staunchly repressive. Guam feels angry. The tension between the locals and the military has spilled over into the psyche of the nation. The taxi driver who takes us to our overnight hotel warns me about the drug-related violence on the island. He tells me that smugglers and mules use Guam as an intermediary between the US and other markets. 'It wasn't always like this,' he says with a heavy heart. I can see the sadness in his eyes in the rear-vision mirror.

Our stay in Guam is short, and we are soon back at the airport en route to our final destination. The plane is small and filled to capacity with returning residents and divers seeking manta rays, who will head onward from Yap to the larger island of Palau.

As Yap comes into view, the sun reflects off the sea, blinding me through the plane window as I anticipate touch down. The plane descends, and I feel a familiar sense of excitement and apprehension about landing somewhere new.

Yap is the most undiscovered land I have ever explored. There is little information available about the island and its people beyond that it operates under very traditional values and maintains a strong cultural identity untarnished by the West. Most websites talk about the island's historic use of stone money, its strict traditions, and the high level of modesty required of the local women.

My decision to visit Yap was not exactly typical of my other off-the-beaten-track adventures. I simply started at the letter Z in the index of an old-fashioned atlas and worked backwards until I found the name of a place I had never heard of. Yap it was.

On landing we disembark on to the hot tarmac. We walk over to a building that has chicken wire for security and two wooden desks in the middle of the room – passport control. The environment in the terminal is chatty and friendly although the language is unfamiliar. Around us, our fellow passengers all appear to be returning Yapese. All the other Western travellers who boarded our flight in Guam have remained on board, awaiting the onward journey to Palau.

We wait as a tractor and trailer stacked high with boxes, crates and plastic-wrapped objects of all sizes is offloaded on to the floor of the baggage area. Just a small number of suitcases are visible among the boxed items. I look for my backpack, filled with essential supplies for the days ahead, including flashlights for our thatched-hut accommodation that has no power or running water. As the last suitcase is picked up, I realise my backpack is absent. My essential items are now limited to the things I packed in my carry-on luggage.

Continental Airlines staff are jovial and apologetic about my missing luggage. They are quick to confirm that it's not lost – it was merely lower priority than the perishable cargo essential for locals. It is hard to argue with their logic. I watch as boxes of food are collected and carried above the heads of locals to waiting pickup trucks. The airline hands over a USD 200 voucher and wishes me well. My bag will be delivered on the next inward flight in seven days' time.

This potentially difficult situation soon becomes somewhat entertaining. We jump on the back of a truck heading to Colonia, the main village centre. I was told I would be able to buy essential supplies for the week ahead at the YCA general store – the only shop on the island with air conditioning and electricity due to a petrol generator that runs 24 hours a day.

When I enter the store I approach a member of staff to ask about my airline voucher and what I can use it for. She replies with an exaggerated, almost Texan twang, 'Honey, you can buy anything your heart desires, but we don't give change.' I decide underwear is probably the best place to start. I walk past hardware supplies, gaudy plastic weaved baskets and rows of dried packaged food to find the clothing section – I use the term 'clothing' loosely as a catch-all for items made to be worn by humans. The humans who shop here must be all sizes and occupations. There are uniforms with brands removed, sarongs so heavily starched that they make a sound when I touch them and what look like real police hats. The underwear department is in short supply – there are two options. The first is an itsy-bitsy lace thong, and the second is what could only be described as bloomers, made for someone at least twice my size and three times my age. On Yap, women typically walk around their villages topless but their thighs stay covered at all times as a required form of modesty.

I go to the men's section to see if it presents any more suitable choices. I am soon armed with a collection of men's underwear

– my time in Yap will be an altogether new clothing experience for me!

On our second day in Yap, we have a chance meeting with a local consulate general's wife. We instantly connect. After an initial conversation, she offers to show us her island, the place she calls home. Danka is technically a foreigner like we are; she's a blonde-haired, blue-eyed Slovakian, and she is a funny, smart and passionate advocate for her adopted island. She tells me in the first few minutes of meeting me that I will leave Yap a different person.

She is right.

Back home in New Zealand, I had two young children who were my world, and a job that was all-consuming. As my career had progressed, I'd faced the trauma that all working parents do: how to balance the time between work and family commitments? When my sons were young, technology had many limitations, including slow and unreliable internet and high costs of adoption. Parent-friendly work hours, school pick-ups and working from home were technical impossibilities and the conversation about the benefits of flexible working was still two decades away.

I found myself setting the alarm clock earlier and earlier. Before I knew it, my day started at 4 am with a run down the rural gravel road near my house in the pitch-black darkness, accompanied by my chocolate Labrador. I knew I was tired but as time went on I stopped recognising tiredness, as I had nothing left to compare it to. I would leave home before 5.30 am to be in the office after 6 am, just so I could get through my work and make it home in time to have dinner with my family.

My exhaustion came to a head when I found myself unable to complete the drive up the unsealed gravel road to my house. It was not uncommon for me to resort to playing loud music, putting my windows down and even pinching myself to stay awake. But even with this range of interventions, I sometimes ran out of ways to keep my eyes open. On these occasions, I would park at the side of the road with a five-minute alarm set to give me enough of a power nap to safely drive the final 2 kilometres to be with my family.

My friends were facing their own versions of exhaustion, and I noticed common patterns emerge. Some went AWOL, others discovered health issues and many faced the breakdown of relationships. As technology enabled us to do more, we found it harder and harder to find time in our days to rest.

In hindsight I now know the exhaustion you feel during the years you raise young children is profound. A continual lack of quality sleep, especially when you're looking after children who don't sleep through the night, is significantly more tiring than a few late nights. I have so much sympathy for working parents of babies and young children. Today, as technology erodes even more of our days and we fixate for longer on our screens, we are starting to lose sight of the need for free, uncommitted time.

I think of my future, the futures of my team, my children and future grandchildren, and I wonder how and when we will learn to carve out time away from screens and constant stimulus so that we have time to imagine, create and dream. Human capacity is immense, but not if our minds are so full and so busy that we lose sight of when things are out of balance. When I step out of my comfort zone to discover new cultures and unfamiliar customs, I'm reminded that there is a big wide world waiting to be discovered. What if the people we love don't know or don't recognise the need to sometimes break away from technology to reset their outlook? What if people become so busy being constantly busy that they truly start to believe there is no other way to live?

Covid-19 broke the world on many levels. We all had dreams and aspirations that were shelved and significant life events that simply couldn't take place. There are few people who haven't experienced a Zoom funeral or a live broadcast wedding since 2020. These events are meant as substitutes for the real thing, but we all know they are not. When we cannot grieve properly, and when we can't wrap our arms round the people we love, the impact is greater than a missed event. We try to adjust to life through a camera, where engagement is not anything like the real world. In the real world, we might see the twitch in the corner of the mouth of a friend who is fighting back tears as we reach to embrace them. In the real world, we have conversations at the watercooler that solve real problems. In the real world, collaborating round a table with sheets of paper and sticky notes brings a sense of belonging and value. If our days are filled with virtual experiences, do we forget the sense of joy we get from participating in live events and togetherness?

We all know that we spend too much time on our devices and not enough time in intimate conversations. But we are getting scarily good at convincing ourselves that a life lived through screens is nearly the same as, or perhaps even better than, the real thing. We are social creatures – we always have been and we always will be. Life is best when it's shaped by feelings, thoughts and emotions that develop when we immerse ourselves in sounds, smells, touches, tastes and sights. I may be the cheer captain for smart technology, but not if it means we supplement our lives with doses of digital to feel alive.

## Arriving when you're meant to

We travel around Yap with Danka in her beat-up 1980s car, driving on the island's only sealed road and exploring the villages and communities dotted around the coastline. As we drive I can't help but wonder how we ensure our children's view of the world is not based on what they see on a screen.

In Yap, the fear of outsiders is tangible, based on stories passed down the ages of time. Danka explains that the villagers are deeply suspicious of new arrivals. Even people from other local villages are required to carry a large leaf as a symbol of peace.

It is reassuring to be in a place where technology hasn't influenced tradition, where I am only welcome on terms that were negotiated in a previous time, by long-passed descendants who knew nothing about the need to rank well on Tripadvisor.

We park Danka's car at the border of a village and pass through beautifully trimmed hedges, then we follow a stone-paved footpath to meet the locals in the village house. Once formalities have been exchanged, I discover our presence is warmly welcomed and we are asked to sit and join the villagers to chew betel leaf and talk in a mix of English and improvised sign language.

The deep-red-stained teeth of the villagers doesn't exactly sell me on the virtues of betel-leaf chewing, but I am happy to sit quietly with the local women and listen to their unfamiliar language and the sounds of the village. There is significant laughter as the school-aged children arrive home in their blue and red wrapped fabric sarongs, the common uniform of the island's schools. There is a quiet chewing sound from the elders who sit on the ground wearing their hibiscus-fibre loincloths and long grass skirts. Words and conversation are much more deliberate than in the Western world, and the sense of turn-taking flows in a naturally forming rhythm. The quiet words of conversation are like music against the backdrop of the water lapping on the shoreline.

Here in the middle of the vast grouping of islands in Micronesia, even the concept of money reflects a different time and place. Yap's stone money has been traded for centuries; the first stone money is thought to have been quarried from Palau as far back as 125 AD. Legend has it that the Yapese attempted to take the stones from Palau across the 400-kilometre ocean journey to Yap in handcrafted canoes. Many were unsuccessful, but those who completed the five-day journey placed their stone money at the entrance of the village to symbolise strength and wealth. The stones are still there today.

One of the most highly valued currencies on the island is called a *gaw*, a necklace formed of shells and whale teeth. Reserved for the chiefs who hold rank in the villages, these necklaces are not on public display. *Yar,* or the local shell money, is also valued as a form of trade, a gift for very specific life events, including marriage proposals, and the purchase of traditional healing or medicinal products. The simplicity of trading with items that are valued by their rarity is not unfamiliar in any part of the world, but it feels a very long way from digital items like non-fungible tokens or Bitcoin, which trade on risk, volatility and the willingness of the open market to determine the price.

So much of our lives in developed markets revolves around money and payments. Even a few years ago there was very little indication of how quickly cryptocurrencies and new financial systems built on the blockchain would shape the way we think about currencies and cash. As global US dollar reserves reduce, and as countries including China, Russia and Sweden look to deploy government digital currencies, pulling physical notes or coins from our wallets for payment is certainly facing its final days.

From day one in Yap, I immediately felt the benefit of living a simpler life. I could feel the pace of the day in minutes, not hours. We could talk without haste, eat without looking at a clock and move through the day without the pressure of time. On one occasion, as we drove between villages, Danka's car chugged a little before coming to a complete stop. At home, breaking down at the side of the road would have been stressful, but we barely stopped our conversation to acknowledge what was happening. Danka simply turned to me, shone her big Slovakian smile and said we had run out of petrol.

She was right not to be concerned, after all, running out of petrol on an island road is a lot less stressful than running out of petrol mid-air in a Cessna. My mind went back to an earlier conversation we'd had, about the fact there were only a handful of petrol stations across the entire island. Nightfall was closing in, and I wondered how we would source the petrol for the journey home. Before I could form the words to ask, Danka opened her door and went to the boot to get a petrol can.

As we walked down the beaten-earth road, I asked Danka if the host village where we were staying would be offended if I was late for dinner. Danka told me that there was no concept of 'late' on the island. You simply arrived when you did.

Again I realised that my internal scheduling tool was still fully operational even though there wasn't a single thing on the island that had to be aligned with a particular time. On Yap, needing to be somewhere didn't exist. You simply lived for the moment.

We approached a village, where the smell of smoke from an improvised fish smoker constructed from an oil drum filled the air. Two young boys jostled together, rotating a handle to turn the drum with the fish inside. We waved our leaves as a sign of peace and after a series of false starts we found a middle-aged teacher from the local school who was keen to help us.

After a brief conversation in broken English, we handed over the fuel can and sat with a growing group of women who smiled with red betel-leaf-stained teeth as they prepared a pile of taro for the evening meal. We sat cross-legged on the ground with them as they spoke and laughed together with words we couldn't understand, but we felt welcome, as though our presence was an everyday occurrence.

It didn't take long for a group of young boys to appear with the fuel can filled with petrol. They handed it over to a female elder, who presented it to us with a cheeky smile. I reached into my pocket and passed her a small bundle of notes in payment for the petrol. Initially she refused, but after my subtle insistence, she smiled and tucked the money away in her skirt. She called to one of the girls to wrap a small bundle of fish and taro in a taro leaf for us to take away.

The simplicity of this exchange stayed with me for weeks after I returned home. It reminded me that no matter how busy we are, if we don't stop for quiet interaction we'll miss the beauty of what it means to be human. We'll miss what words don't say and what the quiet can tell us.

Escaping to different cultures, to locations where life is slower and less influenced by consumption and Western ways, continues to be an important part of my life. I have learned more about value, generosity and business on these journeys than I ever have sitting in a conference or attending a course. One of the bravest things you can do is to step out of familiar settings and routines to enable your heart, mind and spirit to experience something that makes you feel and see the world through a different lens. Not all learning is controlled by the brain, and not all of life can be fulfilled by the constant replay of what we already know.

Right now the world is looking at and experimenting with new economic models. Constant growth at all costs no longer suits a world bracing for the unprecedented challenges of inequality, climate change and growing demand for natural resources. Solving these problems will require businesses to welcome and embrace diverse perspectives and views. We need to bring all generations to the decision-making table in a meaningful way, and we need to recognise the rich diversity of people in the world who've developed an inseparable connection with their environment, and who have understood the strength of a cohesive community for many thousands of years.

In the world's most remote tribes, traditional cultures and communities, each person plays a role in maintaining equilibrium.

There is so much that Western cultures can learn from knowledge that has been developed over many multiple generations and across centuries to better inform our relationship with the future. We need to take responsibility for the source of our decisions and the influences on our views, as not all new information is good, true or useful. Sometimes we must look back to find the clarity we need to move forward.

Gaining a new perspective by venturing into the unknown brings many unexpected rewards. One of the most beneficial things you can do to live a life without regrets is take time to reflect and think.

If I had the ability to push pause on the constant travelator of modern life I would spend a few months each year in a place like Yap. I find myself in many debates, on both the utopian and dystopian sides, about technology and the modern world. I have learned that we need to find our own equilibrium. Nothing is truly binary. In our world and our time, so much of what we do is subjective and intangible. There is no one model of an ideal future, as our experiences vary dramatically from person to person. What makes one person happy is deeply personal and cannot be transferred. While we all need to feel loved, contentment depends on many personal needs. I know I need quiet to feel truly alive. I can find a quiet spot in a park, or visit a hidden coffee house in a bustling city, or read on a deserted beach. The balance of fast and slow, macro and micro, big and small has given me perspective and meaning as I grapple with a life that feels faster and increasingly disconnected.

I sometimes awake to a new day with the overwhelming need for space. Those who know me well recognise that my annual trips to off-the-beaten-track places are my way of finding quiet and time to reflect on my life. Discovering a new country off grid and off calendar is my happy place. It isn't just the adjustment to life offline; it's living life without a sense of urgency.

As a child, my happy place was creating and crafting my own make-believe world, where there was no sense of time, no knowledge of technology and no understanding of boredom. Today, just to find time to reflect and relax takes preparation. We have become so good at filling our days that quiet time becomes an entry in our diaries.

My trips away provide deep clarity and perspective, as I get to see life through the eyes of others. Each journey I take to another culture brings me a deeper understanding of my own role and the purpose I can bring. Being away from home comforts allows my mind to be filled with new inputs, firing up new neurons as my brain forms new pathways.

## The gift of something unexpected

In 2018 I travelled alone through Oman during the sacred month of Ramadan. It was 40-plus degrees Celsius, and most Omanis were isolating inside their homes, away from the unrelenting heat. Businesses were closed for Ramadan so the roads across the country were empty apart from lone delivery trucks moving foods and goods between cities.

One day, a week into my trip, I was fortunate to stop in a mountain village where a group of Bedouin tribeswomen were selling their wares at a small marketplace. Bedouin women wear a very distinctive traditional face mask that's almost Batman-esque in its appearance, and the effect is totally striking as their eyes shine out from the surrounds of black cloth.

Bedouin women are famously shy and reserved, but they invited me to sit with them and their children. I sat on the ground and joined their world. With no common language, we shared ideas through gestures and signs. They were selling beaded necklaces, coloured pastes and braided threads. I tried to purchase a beautifully woven amulet but they insisted that I receive it as a gift. Their children practised English words with me, laughing as they stumbled over unfamiliar vowels. Tea was shared and we connected for a moment in time with our made-up language of gestures and sounds.

The owner of a nearby shop invited me into his store, which was filled with beaten copper vessels, carved wooden camels, local delicacies and a very significant display of bandoliers, the leather belt accessory designed to hold large numbers of individual bullets. With limited English, he asked if he could recite a poem to me and asked me to film him. I stood in his small shop with my phone camera held up to capture his words. He sat on a tapestry-covered chair wearing his dishdasha, the long white gown worn by local men, and he had a long white beard and a white mussar on his head.

He faced my camera and spoke to me in the local Arabic dialect. The rhythmic tones of his gentle voice suggested a heartfelt message. I desperately wished I could understand his words. It wasn't until I returned home to New Zealand and showed the video to an Arabic-speaking colleague that I found out what he'd said. My colleague watched the video intently then almost keeled over in laughter. Apparently I had missed out on the proposal of a lifetime. Rather than accept the store owner's very generous offer to stay in this traditional Omani village as his wife, I had simply thanked him for his words and walked out of his life.

When I left the village, I took a silver-and-turquoise bracelet from my wrist and gifted it to the oldest of the women in the group. Her eyes looked deeply into mine and she thanked me without a word being exchanged. It was a moment I will remember forever: two women from different sides of the planet sharing a bond of curiosity and respect. I still wear her handmade bracelet and I hope she wears mine.

The things that we value most in life are sometimes the things we least expect. I look back at photos from that day and feel a sense of calm and absolute peace. I didn't find out the name of the Bedouin woman who gave me the bracelet, but if I did I would tell her I carry her sense of grace and serenity in my heart. She made a difference in my life in a way she will never know.

I wish more people would travel to lesser-known countries or regions, where life is not designed around the tourist dollar. So much in our everyday lives is designed to make things easier, to fit into our diaries better, to ensure we can keep our appointments. One day in an unfamiliar environment can feel like a week's worth of growth. Time moves slowly when you're not watching the clock. New experiences are critical for human development.

When so many holiday locations look and feel just like the next, we have removed the opportunity to learn and feel new things during our visits. So many people repeatedly head back to the same holiday resorts, where they enjoy food and activities like those they have at home. As my children have grown they've joined me on my journeys, and they too have developed a love of the unfamiliar. Maybe these adventures have helped me to trust in the unknown and made me more comfortable with change. Life is best when it's lived through all senses. It helps us develop courage, and in time we learn to understand risk in a much more balanced way.

In a book on the future, my reflections on travel and my experiences in unfamiliar lands may seem out of place. But I see connections in everything we choose to do in our lives and every situation has something to teach us. I've always been an active relaxer – I like to get up when it's still dark and to make the most of every day.

Billions of people share the experience of living and breathing on this planet, but no two people experience the same life. I try hard not to make assumptions or to presume that people want or need the same things as me. I know my world the only way I can – through my eyes and ears. When we experience new systems and processes, we can find meaning and make decisions based on our known understanding.

It is important that we learn to recognise when our mental, physical and emotional reserves are operating on empty and life no longer feels joyous. The relentless grind to squeeze all of our commitments into a given week, month or year sometimes means that we run out of time to find space to live. I can't profess to have a great work–life balance, or to get enough sleep, but I do know when I need time out.

Sometimes I will plan an escape weeks before I go and other times I will urgently need to find space. One night I was sitting at home, knowing I was operating on zero reserves, when I booked a flight for the very next morning to Uluru in Australia. As I flew across the desert of red earth and landed in the Northern Territory, I felt freer than I had for weeks.

There is no right or wrong way to find the space you need to clear a busy mind. If you know you're falling into a trap of endless repetition where one day is blending into the next, perhaps it's time to take off the handbrake and go on a little life detour.

## CHAPTER 5

# Chance encounters

## Be open to all things

### Everything – and everyone – is connected

Call it coincidence, fate or even destiny, but a chance meeting with one person can completely change your outlook and even your life. On this strange journey you will often cross paths and collide with people you will assume you have nothing in common with – and you'll be wrong. I'm not convinced that all encounters are accidental. Is it possible that being open to seemingly chance interactions might lead us to discover exactly where we are meant to be heading? Could it be that intuition uses such experiences as a form of live data, and that your brain uses you to make highly informed subliminal decisions that will guide you through life?

The feeling of déjà vu can be euphoric. It delivers an unexpected flash of familiarity that doesn't know where to land. It's the opposite of the feeling that comes with intuition; intuition feels like a precursor of what's to come, whereas déjà vu feels like a flashback. Both senses have a place in life and business, but few professionals are brave enough to admit that gut instinct, or a feeling of unexplainable familiarity, has a part to play in business decision-making.

We are taught that life is tangible, assets are real and business deals follow rules. The official school of thought says we should follow long-established rules and formulas, the logic being that established and proven approaches do not need reinventing. But a different perspective will often provide the clarity we need to truly understand a problem.

Familiarity is one of the strongest emotions we carry. It is the fragrance that reminds you of your old work colleague, or the meal that takes you back to your childhood dining table, or the song that makes you feel 18 again. The surroundings, context and people might be new, but the power of familiarity is visceral and instinctual.

I have learned to trust my intuition, but following a hunch is a journey without a rule book. We've all had moments of meeting someone who feels familiar, even though we've never met them before. It is as though, on some level of consciousness, we build connections based on intangible links that just click. Some of my most memorable conversations have been built on this – a chance conversation on a plane, or at a conference, or over a crowded dinner table. I have also experienced this instant connection with people I have mentored, matchings based on a system far outside of my control.

I have mentored numerous women over the past 20 years. Those who became much more than mentees were people I connected with on a personal level. We could be candid about our doubts and worries, and we formed strong bonds of trust. I see trust as the most powerful connection of all; trusting someone takes an incredible leap of faith. Trust is one of the most significant gifts we can receive and the most dangerous gift to break.

In my early career, I admired people because of their strength. At no time did I build an emotional connection with them. Trust wasn't talked about in the workplace – hierarchies of control were based on power, not relatability. The only female leaders I knew were strong women. They told it as they saw it. If they ever felt pressure in their decision-making, they never showed it. I lived in awe of their presence, the way they strode with conviction to lead the first generation of women to break through the glass ceiling. I have read the memoirs of some of these women, and I realise now their lived realities were often far removed from the stoic front they presented.

When I was younger I thought of people, jobs, places and connections as discrete, standalone things. I didn't give much thought to the interrelationship of the forces that shaped my day and informed my thinking. Only recently have I truly appreciated the concept of systems thinking, evaluating why things happen the way they do or why people act and behave in certain ways. By better understanding the relationship between these many interconnected parts, I can see context and the risks within systems. Understanding the levers of influence and the catalysts for change is a core feature of futures planning, where systems thinking is used to model and predict behaviour.

In relationships, it can sometimes feel as though things unfold according to a predetermined schedule and at other times it feels as though they're out of our control. Premonitions, fate, destiny, unexplained coincidences in our lives: these are the patterns that keep recurring without reason. Many instances can be explained away, such as constantly seeing the exact colour car you have just bought in traffic because of your heightened awareness, but other coincidences are harder to explain.

## Letting things fall into place

Right now, here in 2022, my office is on the ground floor of a building that's literally a stone's throw from my very first New Zealand office, where I had my first business-leadership role nearly 30 years ago. The building has since been demolished and replaced by an apartment complex, but the neighbourhood is still recognisable, even if it has been gentrified. The community is now much more typical of the world in 2022: five-star eateries are mixed in with noodle houses, an e-bike store and a gym that proudly markets its technology as a way to entice me to get me fit.

If you were to lay out my life so far, it would look like a series of interconnecting experiences with similar themes but without any obvious connections. In the early 1990s, when I first returned from overseas and jobs were proving to be elusive, I ended up leading a new organisation in a somewhat unorthodox way. I was still young but my experiences showed a breadth of diverse skills, and this eventually attracted a rather non-traditional employer, at least compared to any employer I had ever seen.

Back in 1992, I was sitting at the bar of a new Cajun restaurant in the Chase Plaza, in the same complex as the NZX. The building was a stronghold of men in dark suits who lunched together, as they speculated about what the market would do next. The restaurant was the new swanky place on the block. It had marble floors and an impressive bar that overlooked an atrium with a human-sized chess board. I had been commissioned by the restaurant to paint a stylised 12-metre-long mural depicting a New Orleans street scene, and I was there hoping to collect payment for my work. The owner of the restaurant was a colourful character who once shared with me that he had done time for robbing a bank in Hawaii. I never saw any evidence to confirm or deny this extraordinary claim, but, judging by the way he operated his businesses, it wouldn't have surprised me.

It was at the bar counter that I happened to meet Iranha. She had a double-barrelled surname and she and her husband lived on a yacht in the harbour. Her claim to fame was that she had dated Elvis. Yes, that Elvis. (Well, that's what the article in a women's magazine said when they profiled her a few weeks after our first meeting, anyway.)

Iranha was a bohemian-chic Californian. When she moved, silver and turquoise jewellery jangled on her wrists. I calculated that she was well into her sixties but her physical agility and fresh, lightly tanned face were like that of a woman in her thirties. I was an instant admirer, and I found myself captivated by her travel stories of life at sea and the lifestyle she had lived in ports around the world.

Iranha was opening a business. She described it as a clinic for personal development supported by technology, but in a dreamcatcher, kumbaya kind of way. I was intrigued. Over a glass of wine, we talked about her vision and the details of her financial backer, a somewhat controversial plastic surgeon who was looking to diversify his business interests. Every aspect of the business was unfamiliar to me, and the concept behind it felt like something from the future, but my work options were light so I agreed to accept her job offer when, just a few days later, she presented my contract.

Whatever Iranha saw in me that first day in the bar I'm not sure I will ever know. At 21 years old, I was suddenly employed as the centre director of the Quantum Mega Brain Centre. The centre was based upon a new technology that used visual and audio immersion to take people deep into a non-REM state to learn new knowledge. My role was to oversee the centre, working with new clients and connecting with organisations and individuals looking to learn new material, from new languages to building confidence. Maybe this centre, focused on learning, the brain and technology, was the first indication of where my career would take me. It was a million miles away from my world in Turkey, or where I'd thought I was heading, but somehow the promise of being part of something revolutionary captured my imagination.

The Mega Brain Centre was the first place I started to explore the relationship between the decisions we make and the doors that open, as opposed to the comfort of staying on a well-planned and well-executed path. I didn't fully know it then, but I am comfortable with ambiguity and letting things fall into place. I had no idea where the role would take me, or how the business would even be received in the market, but I knew I wanted to work alongside Iranha.

Nearly three decades have passed since I left the role, and in that time I have experienced many different types of job and worked for many different types of boss. None of the people I have met were like Iranha. She was almost ethereal. She would float into the office, bright eyes shining, her skin always radiant and her flowing dresses skimming just centimetres off the floor. Her calmness put people at ease. She would answer my questions with her own questions: *How would you solve the problem? What do you think the best option is?* I had never had such trust and responsibility put on me before, but I relished her confidence in my capabilities. I found myself leading a team of people that Iranha had met on her journey across the city. Every member of the team had a story about how they met Iranha.

For the first few months I saw Iranha daily, then weekly, then suddenly, without warning, she and her husband were gone. It was as though she had simply decided that her time there was done. I heard the weather took her and her yacht north – the tropical South Pacific beckoned. Nothing in her life was predetermined or planned; she moved to her own schedule and danced to the beat of her own drum.

After her departure, her vibrant energy soon dissipated and the centre felt overly functional and sterile. The confidence I'd had when she was there disappeared with her, and suddenly the burden of leading a team of people twice my age felt heavy with responsibility.

I tried to build a new culture in her absence, but I couldn't re-establish the energy she'd brought to the organisation. At that moment I fully appreciated that a person brings far more than the experiences and qualifications on their CV. Iranha's ability to connect with others and to put them at ease was almost magical. I was a novice trying hard to build a team culture. I committed to learning how to build trusted, cohesive teams and to support groups of people. I grew to understand that showing up means more than being present.

The centre manager role, with its 6 am starts and late finishes, taught me what it means to carry the weight of a business on your shoulders. I was on the payroll, and I bore no financial risk, but I would lie awake at night worrying about how many people in the organisation relied on me to make good decisions for their livelihoods. The only way I really knew how to build the business was to work harder. Obsessively so.

'Fake it until you make it' became my unspoken mantra. I set a goal of mimicking everything I had observed in successful business people. My suits became better tailored and I traded my flat shoes for uncomfortable heels. I wanted to ensure that no one could see my self-doubt, and that I would look like a leader even if internally I felt like a fraud. I knew I had knowledge gaps to fill, so I read every business book I could get my hands on – this was all in the world before internet, so the things I didn't know could only be supplied through good books and access to smart people.

Many years later I first heard the phrase 'imposter syndrome', and I now recognise this role as centre director was the first time I felt truly out of my depth. Every day I would unlock the front door and force a smile on my face, telling myself it would get easier over time. Perhaps it was my fear of failure or letting others down, or maybe I had just enough confidence to pull myself forward, but I practised and visualised feeling more confident and less like someone who was role-playing.

Has anyone ever had such strong self-belief that they've never doubted their decisions or actions? I must assume so. I like the idea that some people have never faced self-confidence issues, but I wonder if it is sometimes important to step into the unknown feeling as though you don't have all the skills to be there. Perhaps striving to be better leads us to develop our capabilities, and gives us the capacity to better understand others.

I didn't stay long in the centre director role. After Iranha's departure, I realised that the job on its own was not enough to keep me. There was talk of a new owner buying in and a new location in one of the city's swankiest suburbs. I realised that the initial steep learnings and enjoyment I got from leading the organisation through the early stages of its establishment diminished once the repetition of day-to-day operations set in.

## A woman on a mission

Iranha wasn't the only person at the Mega Brain Centre who made a huge impact on my life. My decision to work there also led to one of the most impactful friendships of my life. I had been in my role as centre director for a couple of weeks when a woman just a little older than me arrived to work as the receptionist. From her first day, I loved that her laugh was so contagious. She is one of the few people I have ever met who can see the positive side of almost any scenario.

My office was just across from reception, and I sat in front of a brand-new desktop computer. Up until then I had not had my own computer. In all my previous roles in London and Europe, computers had been task-based processing machines shared by many. The idea of a personal computer, just for me, seemed excessive. While I was eager to learn about technology and automation, my hands-on experience was very limited.

A couple of days after she started, the receptionist noticed that I was not using my computer. She came and asked if I needed any help booting it up. I can only assume she saw the relief in my eyes, as without saying anything further she moved me aside and started typing away. She patiently explained the MS-DOS 5x booting sequence with the new full-screen editor. I watched on, frantically taking notes so I would be able to replicate her commands.

I have learned so much from this one very special person. She is one of the most humble people I have ever met, but more than that she is the most resilient. Even when I first met her she had already experienced so much trauma and abuse inflicted by people she should've been able to trust. We say that bad luck comes in threes, but not in my friend's instance. Her runs of three turned into runs of nine and still they kept coming. In 2014, I was with her in the doctor's office when she was told she had breast cancer and that her breast would need to be removed as soon as possible. As I sat in stony-faced shock, she simply said to the doctor, 'You better take them both off, as I want a gorgeous matching pair when you're done.'

We went out for dinner after the doctor's appointment and I fought back tears. She was the one who told me it would be all right. My heart felt like it was being ripped out of my chest. I cried for my friend. I wondered how she could've been dealt yet another bad hand, and I wondered how many blows one person could receive and still get up to smile at another day.

This friend has been part of my life longer than most. We attended each other's weddings and we watched each other's children grow up. I recently watched as she packed up her car with her daughter and a pile of suitcases when her daughter left home for university. A week later, instead of sitting back and enjoying the quiet of an empty nest, she turned up at my graduate school and enrolled in postgraduate studies. Now she has become a learning monster – she took to her studies like a caffeine addict looking for their first morning brew. Her new mission is to keep learning until she has completely reinvented herself for her next career.

There is no one more inspirational than a woman on a mission, and no one more mission-led than this remarkable friend. I suspect she is totally oblivious to how many people watch on in awe of her ability to get back up each time life tries to bring her down.

## Coming full circle

Let me take you back to today. I am sitting in my Tech Futures Lab office, just 100 metres down the road from where I was the centre director for the Mega Brain Centre nearly 30 years ago. I realise my circle of life is big and small. Maybe I operate on two levels by choice – macro and micro, local and global. I realise now that I don't need to choose between being the international jet-setter and the local technologist; I am both and neither. We all operate under different modes as time, circumstance and chance dictates. We are products of circumstance and connection. To one person you might be the coach of the netball team, to another you might be the head of the department. You might be a wife, husband, mum or sister. Our career choices are just a small part of who we are and who we become. Great leaders know that the stripes you earn at work are not transferable to other contexts. Respect is acknowledging that every situation has a different set of rules and norms.

I am infinitely thankful for the many coincidences that brought me on the journey to where I am today. Would I still be doing this if I hadn't met my friend, and she hadn't shown me how to boot up my first personal computer in 1992? Would I still be in New Zealand if Iranha hadn't connected with me in a bar all those years ago? Whether it is fate, destiny or just good luck, many of the things that shape our lives come from chance meetings.

We learn more about ourselves when times are tough than we ever will when life runs smoothly. Life doesn't dish out adverse experiences in tidy groups of three, and nor does it fairly distribute challenges. What we do in moments of adversity, when all the cards are on the table and there is nothing left to do but to be honest, is what makes us who we are.

I'm not the leader I was in my early career. Gone are the power plays and the illusion of strength. These days I sign off my emails to staff with kisses and hugs. I share my fears and ambitions widely. I learned my leadership skills from women much stronger than me, but I prefer the new me, the one who often gets it wrong but who will try to put things right. We all have the capacity to evolve and to change the way we learn, lead and interact. One of the greatest joys in life is looking back and seeing just how far you've come.

## CHAPTER 6

# The future is digital

Evolve like your future depends on it

### The dawn of the digital world

I often wish I could transport myself back to certain moments in my life to better understand what younger me was thinking. What was going through my head at the time? Why did I choose one path over another? It feels unfair that our brains don't come with backup systems that would allow us to replay moments with full clarity, in the same way we look back at photos and videos of special events.

While my career has been shaped by technology and digital advances, I visualise my life as a series of creative endeavours, starting with the non-stop craft projects I worked on as a child, through to my love today of creating beautiful spaces. If you'd used my high-school subject choices as an indicator of where I would eventually land, you might've assumed that I was destined to become a designer. With the single exception of my interest in maths, I've always focused on the creation of beautiful artefacts, from furniture to murals, montages to fashion.

I was 20 when technology thoroughly captured my attention; I could see the potential and how the world was changing and I was a convert. The 1990s were technology's playtime. Corporate tech companies grew quickly and rose to dominate the market. Nokia, PlayStation, Nintendo, Microsoft, Linux, Adobe, Netscape and even PalmPilot became household names. The superheroes of the world were no longer movie stars but tech founders, and everywhere I went I heard conversations about the knowledge economy and how technology was changing the world.

I had one other very important superhero, who was behind the scenes to the outside world but absolutely front of mind to me. This person was my mother.

In the years between starting her family and when I returned home from Europe, my mother had single-handedly forged her own significant career. She started by setting up travel and tourism companies, and this led to her driving change in the fields of travel and tourism education. She saw change unfolding in front of her: qualifications requirements for all travel and tourism employees were changing, and computerised airline booking and information systems were moving away from paper-based ticketing to global computerised ticketing systems. She recognised that the travel and tourism working environment needed to be stimulated through learning and new qualifications. In isolation from my mother's career, it could be assumed that I fell into technology and education coincidentally, but in reality I was only doing what my mother had already responded to in her sector. Having set up highly successful travel and tourism schools and diploma programmes within two existing learning institutes, she then embarked on her own entrepreneurial journey as the founder of Media Design School.

I joined Media Design School in 1999 as the general manager, when it was still a start-up, and I would stay there for 14 years. My role was focused on the creative technologies sector and the development of students who wanted to enter the emerging film sector as visual-effects artists and animators. Traditional paper-based designers were swapping their pens for software, digitising their creative processes to feed the growing demand for digital content. New sectors, including graphic design and data visualisation, were gaining momentum. Businesses focused on the future of entertainment were testing and commercialising new products. Interactive screens, augmented reality, online games, and software that could mimic human behaviour were all spun out of research labs and thrust into the limelight.

My learning curve was steep, as I was learning as fast as the sector was. I had to navigate and understand new software, as well as the ever-changing hardware, as the war between the tech companies pushed innovation faster and faster. The New Zealand film industry was propelled to the frontier of entertainment as a world leader in visual effects. Our country's reputation as a nation of sheep farmers was suddenly replaced by a reputation for high-end visual effects thanks to the films being designed in our technology- and talent-rich studios. The Lord of the Rings trilogy was in production and the entire country was trying to understand this new, innovative sector.

I participated in many global trade exhibitions where the digitalisation of products and services dominated. In particular, the annual SIGGRAPH (Special Interest Group on Computer Graphics and Interactive Techniques) conference in the US presented hall after hall of organisations that were changing the world with tech. SIGGRAPH was a catch-all for anything that was leading edge in the tech world. Technology was disrupting almost every business process, and the internet soon became a platform for people to connect in ways that literally changed the course of the world.

As I watched the world change in front of my eyes, I couldn't shake the sense that businesses should be paying more attention to what was happening. The technology industry started to build collectives dedicated to specific technologies, from film and computer games, to multimedia and future technologies. The entire tech and creative sectors were in growth mode as a multitude of highly innovative organisations worked to put New Zealand on the map of global tech. Each sector niche formed associations, which were supported by advisory boards and government reference groups. I joined as many sector organisations as I could, from the games industry to the screen industry, to software and tech-hardware association boards. I committed as much time as I could to being part of a conversation that was shaping our country and propelling New Zealand forward as a serious creative-technology hub.

In these meetings, I was surrounded by some of the greatest local innovators of our time. Technology gurus from the different sectors were pushing hard to make digitalisation part of the fabric of change. When we got together, we talked about the internet, software advances, global trade and new markets. We imagined the promise of super-fast internet replacing dial-up, we celebrated global releases of local innovations, and we obsessed over the lack of local talent to support the tech sector's growth. Twenty-three years ago the tech landscape was still in its infancy, and studios, labs and companies made up a tight-knit community of innovators shaping our country's future.

By the time the new millennium rolled round, tech companies had Immigration New Zealand on speed dial. Bringing in highly skilled technology experts from offshore was the only way to meet the demand for growth. My focus was still on developing local talent for the film, visual-effects and games industries, but I could see a near future when technology would jump from the edges of economic activity to the very core of all business functions.

From 2000 to 2013, computer-processing speeds increased by around 25 per cent each year. Central processing units (CPUs) went from 800 MHz at the beginning of 2001 to 1.6 GHz in 2002, and to 3.2 GHz by the end of 2003. The first cracks between traditional business practice and future digital practice were beginning to show, and it wasn't only the business world that was experiencing steep changes – the world of music was reimagined overnight with the launch of the iPod and iTunes.

Like many people, I still have an iPod with a lifetime's worth of CDs stored on it. And, as with most redundant technology, I no longer have a way to play it. It sits as a relic in the junk drawer. The speed with which one technology is replaced by another is one of the key disconnects between generations and their different understandings of what's possible. Case in point: not long ago I was speaking to a group that included a large number of children aged ten to 12 years. I was talking about the evolution of technology when I mentioned the iPod in passing. A young girl in the front row immediately threw up her arms and began waving them wildly to catch my attention. I stopped my presentation and asked this young woman what her question was. She stood proudly and told me that I was wrong. There was no such thing as an iPod – maybe I meant an iPad? It took a moment for her statement to compute in my mind. This was early 2020. Most people had stopped using their iPods by 2007, when the first iPhone came out. The girl was 11 years old – iPod technology had entered the market well before she was even born. It was yet another reminder that young people see the world through a very different lens.

As an outsider looking in, it might be hard to fathom how my career pivoted from fashion to technology and education when I didn't have any formal training. Indeed, if you compare my career to traditional career development and formal learning, then my journey will make little sense. It turns out, everything in my life has come down to timing. When technology and the internet first became accessible to consumers, there were no qualifications to teach you how to create multimedia or how to develop websites. Everyone in the business was self-taught, hacking systems and self-educating to see how things worked. The film industry was awash with creatives transferring their analogue craft of illustration to 3D modelling and animation. Storytellers were writing concepts for computer games and software engineers were writing new types of code to bring interactive experiences to life. Few people had more than a few years' experience in computer graphics, and the demand for new content to feed the pipelines of the film and gaming industries was growing exponentially. In the early years between 1998 and 2005, the entire tech industry was experimental. There was a workaround for every problem, and if something couldn't be solved immediately we knew that within a short period of time computer-processing capabilities and software advancements would make new options possible.

The early 2000s progressed and I was deep within the hustle of the emerging world. My colleagues were recruited from around the globe to bring their expertise from some of the most advanced creative-technology markets. Media Design School became one of New Zealand's first hubs for innovators who led change from the frontline. No part of the sector was traditional. There were no rules. It was an industry formed by highly creative, intelligent and visionary people who wanted to change the world. It was fast-paced, disruptive and intoxicating. No one cared where people came from, or what experience they had – all anyone needed to know was whether you could see beyond what was possible to imagine the future. Innovation became the most coveted skill of the time, as the sector pushed boundaries and created new opportunities.

I soon recognised that I loved to be around the people in the tech sector. There was a delightful mix of eclectics and mavericks, including those who'd been tarnished with labels because of their nonconformist way of thinking. This group of misfits, boffins and geeks became my favourite tribe and my most supportive collective. They saw possibilities that most traditional thinkers could not see. They held the superpower of understanding systems change, adoption curves and technological convergence. These characteristics are still undervalued in most mainstream systems, where conformity and predictability are celebrated over divergent thought.

Once I was embedded in this tribe of diverse contributors, I saw the merits of collaboration and project-based teams. I understood how bringing a collection of diverse thinkers to the table had the ability to drive change much faster than teams of similarly skilled people who lack the ability to think differently. It was the first time I experienced the benefits of true diversity of thought within a team. I have never looked back. Today my organisations are rich in diversity – that includes cultural, gender, age, experience and skills. I wouldn't have it any other way.

## The adoption curve

To understand where the world is heading, you need to understand the adoption curve of technology. Each new technology is first adopted by innovators, followed by early adopters, then the early majority, then the late majority, all the way through to the laggards, the people who are the most resistant to new technologies. There are many contributing factors as to why some people are late to the party, including ease of access, affordability, relevance and perceived importance. But the adoption curve helps us understand how risk moves, from the risk of getting in too early to the risk of adopting new skills too late. In the world today, too many highly competent people defer picking up a new technology until it's too late. What would happen if you woke up tomorrow and your entire industry had been digitised, in the same way that film, music or media has been? Would you have time to catch up or would the wave of disruption be too big to navigate?

When I work with organisations advising them on the future of technologies, I focus on the curve of adoption. Most new emerging technologies, from electric cars to solar panels to virtual reality, predominantly start with the super-wealthy. Our ability to be 'always on' has changed the adoption curve from being steady and contained, to becoming rapid and far-reaching, as most technologies now piggy-back off core technology that already exists – like the smartphone and internet connectivity. Young people relying on technology is a massive motivating factor for tech companies – young people number in the billions, and their buying power is spurring the development of new hardware and software. The reach and hype of products that meet the youth market can dominate within weeks of launch. You only need to think about the massive overnight uptake of Pokémon GO, Minecraft and Fortnite to understand how powerful this market share is.

It's important that I re-emphasise the rapid rate of change we are now experiencing, because there has never been a more important time to understand the shifts your career and life will face in the next few years. We are all at the start line of the world's biggest technology-innovation-adoption race, and keeping up will take a commitment to being match fit.

One silver lining of Covid-19 has been the further democratisation of access to knowledge. Education is no longer limited to campuses; the geographic borders between students and institutions have been removed as institutes move online and learning becomes available to many more people. In addition, the options for learning are broader and more compelling than ever before. Just a simple scan of the programme offerings at world-class institutions shows a huge range of subject options: flying car and autonomous flight engineer; CRISPR gene-editing; AI for healthcare; machine learning with TensorFlow; data structures and algorithms; activation and retention strategy; hybrid cloud engineer; ethical hacker; Android Kotlin developer. Schools of knowledge have become fragmented as technology converges with other fields, including science and engineering, and together they morph into new areas of expertise.

I am so excited to see how much more accessible knowledge and contemporary information has become for those who seek it. The historic barriers of extraordinarily high tuition fees are being disbanded and replaced with higher levels of accessibility, including the ability to learn fully online. The only thing needed now is a commitment to start learning.

## Dancing to a different beat

In 2013, when I founded The Mind Lab, I initially focused on teaching technology to young students. What I didn't realise at the time of the launch was that there were literally thousands of families fighting the education system for their children. I define these children as quirky, but the system defines them as failures because of their inability to follow logic or to learn in the same way or at the same pace as the 'majority'. The so-called majority is a powerful collective of people who think and react in uniform ways, and entry to this exclusive club is only permitted if you happen to fall within a narrow band of 'normal'.

In the early years of schooling, students attach themselves to like-minded people who typically look and live in very similar ways to themselves, and so the club begins. By the time students have become adolescents and moved on to higher education, age-based connections are deepened by subject-based connections in the form of chosen subjects. The sporty kids hang together, as do the musical kids and the science kids.

Even students who didn't go to a tertiary institution will be aware of the rise of social cliques based on a person's postcode, ethnicity, educational achievement or interests. Excluded from these collectives are the people who cannot be defined by traditional groupings. These individuals move to their own beat, either because they are ambivalent towards established collectives or unafraid to be themselves. These individuals can often see solutions or possibilities where others can't – they're the people who change the world and create a future no one could've imagined. These were the people I worked alongside as the technology sector soared.

Show me a game-changing technological advancement that hasn't been developed by someone the mainstream would define as 'a little bit different'. Big ideas, it turns out, need big-thinking nonconformists. Our need to fit people into neatly defined boxes works well for the compliant workers of the world, but it does little to create the diverse environments where innovation thrives. Innovators are the world's changemakers. They are the people who will solve our problems and improve our planet. If I had my way, they would be celebrated as the heroes of the world.

When I look back, I realise I have never really left my technology tribe. They were and are the people who inspire me; they're constantly adapting and evolving to address new challenges. When I'm surrounded by business people from traditional sectors, such as finance or law, I still feel like the young me – the introvert who would rather hide behind the couch or my mum's skirt. I try to rationalise these thoughts, but they don't really make sense. What I do know is that people who like predictability and the organised processes of most business environments don't always understand my way of thinking about the world.

Judgement doesn't have to be overt to be felt. In my tech world, I am surrounded by kindred spirits who like to mix things up and build new ways to solve problems. My earliest heroes may be long forgotten, but my tech heroes are superhuman, turning zeroes and ones into codes that make the world a better place.

## Building a bridge between yesterday and tomorrow

My career was formed through a combination of the right time and right place. I developed my understanding of software and hardware on the job, and through my networks. Today, in 2022, we are part of a new time and place. One that is much more technological and digital than the world we knew even two years ago. If your career is already established, now is the time to build a bridge between your career of the past and your career of the future. Every single industry is facing the effect of new entrants who are developing businesses built on new advances and the connection to smartphones and the internet.

Finding time to learn, talk and read outside of work and family commitments is hard, but understanding how to keep your career on track is an incredibly valuable undertaking. In fact, it's crucial if you want to ensure your career will continue to grow and develop.

I'm incredibly thankful that I fell into the world of tech just as it exploded into mainstream adoption. I am grateful that, from the day I first dipped my toes in, every day has been a learning day. Mostly I am thankful for what technology has enabled me to do.

Popular culture will tell you that the robots are coming and your job is at risk. My view is that automation and artificial intelligence will most likely impact your tasks rather than your role, in the same way we now sign documents electronically and collaborate on cloud-hosted shared files. Many of our tasks will be processed by algorithms. However, it is our responsibility to lean into new ways of processing functions and mobilising systems so that our customers, clients and community can benefit from the lower costs and productivity gains of tech-enabled businesses.

Like any programme where behavioural change is required, start your journey into the future with small steps and fixed goals. Better still, team up with others and learn together. The information, courses and online events dedicated to the future of work are almost limitless. The only barrier to your career progression and the future-proofing of your next phase in life is you.

## CHAPTER 7

# Allies and adversaries

Choose trust and collaboration
over hierarchy and power

## In search of a better work culture

We tend to expect that any one organisation is much like another, so when you find yourself in a company that plays by very different rules, or that demonstrates a high tolerance of bad behaviour, it can be soul-destroying. From the outside, it is very difficult to know whether the public perception of an organisation will match the internal reality. Perfectly scripted marketing fronts and curated social media feeds share little about an organisation's inner workings.

We spend much of our lives working. Whether you head into the office every day, or you work remotely at one end of a Zoom call, the organisation you put your energy into and represent becomes a significant part of your life. As such, it's critical that your values are well aligned with those of the organisation you work for. Most importantly, when you are not at work it is reasonable to expect that you think of your work with a sense of pride and accomplishment.

Interrelationships between people can be complex. Human interaction assumes a certain amount of known and predictable behaviours: we learn to anticipate reactions and we use the same rules of expectation when others engage with us – or so we assume. It's confronting when an interaction with a colleague, a client or a leader deviates from these known norms or becomes combative, and it can be as disruptive as a weapon being discharged.

Even people known for their sense of fun and carefree nature have bad days. But some bad behaviours stem from ignorance or an inflated sense of self-worth, including age dominating over youth, using the privilege of money and knowledge to overpower others, and using physical intimidation to instil fear. I have witnessed, in the presence of others, how sexual innuendo and the overstepping of boundaries can make a person feel powerless. Throughout my career I have experienced power plays, payments being held back and threats to my reputation used as mechanisms of control. I have seen leaders promote friends or use threats of retaliation to make sure certain actions are done or not done.

We can hold others up or bring them down. If we choose to, we can support the underdog, champion the underrepresented and initiate a different type of work culture.

## The alpha leader

In my life I have identified two types of people who are misunderstood by employers. I've already discussed one – the nonconformist, who is seen as highly unconventional and often overlooked by an employer because of their disarming lack of adherence to expected business norms and their nonstandard approach to the 'system'. The other type runs like poison through an organisation, dispensing their narrative and spreading self-indulgent propaganda to propel themselves to the top. These people are often known internally for their inaction and lack of responsiveness, but they are very good at looking competent, and they sidle up to those who can influence their career progression.

Too often the second group thrives in corporations, where the system is designed to support people with highly competitive natures and high levels of confidence. The nonconformists are scarcely seen in large organisations because they rarely make it beyond the first recruitment hurdle. If a nonconformist is hired, they often stay in the same role for many years as they're repeatedly overlooked for promotions.

Many organisations operate according to the views of alpha personalities and the dominance of charismatic leaders. Hierarchy in many large entities is built on a range of confident personalities and bold behaviours. The most overt demonstrations of power-based control I have seen have occurred in executive teams and governance boards. While my life has mostly been spent outside of corporations, I have spent a considerable amount of time working with executive teams and boards as a technologist and specialist in the future of work. The latter has been the focus of my work since 2016, when I founded Tech Futures Lab. It is in this role, working with external parties, that I have seen and heard the most aggressive and undermining behaviour, including disparaging comments that show bias, ignorance, racism and gender discrimination.

Many businesses elevate or promote individuals who fit the mould of what they perceive to be a successful employee or leader. In some cases, startlingly obvious personality flaws are overlooked or tolerated because of success metrics or the misguided view that the individual's reputation is good for business. And I have met many people in my career who adopted a leadership approach based on control and fear.

In 2012 I was the CEO of Media Design School, which had recently been acquired by a very large international entity. My new boss was based in the US, and they were part of the global executive team. The reach of this large organisation extended across multiple countries and continents. They were well resourced, ambitious and looking to achieve global market dominance.

While my typical working day was unaffected by the new global owners, my work often required me to stay up through the night to be part of long executive calls so that I could participate in meetings in their local time zone. The hardest of these calls ran for eight hours every month, starting at midnight New Zealand Time. At this time the internet was slow, limited, expensive and unreliable. I lived rurally and my total internet threshold each month was just 8 GB. I had to join an internal network for shared documents and phone-in to a shared conference line, so my only option was to take these calls from my city office, 35 kilometres away from my home. So once a month I would stay in my office after everyone had left for the day, find a quiet couch for a few hours of sleep, then wake just before midnight to join a marathon call that would finally wind up just as my staff were arriving to work.

I was part of a team of global CEOs at sister institutes, and we talked frequently about the challenges of deadlines and targets as we consoled each other when we missed yet another family birthday or special gathering. At the airport I would see familiar looks of exhaustion as I scanned my fellow passengers boarding flights alongside me, destined for yet another generic hotel and nondescript meeting room in another high-rise building. When I had the opportunity to be at home I'd look forward to Mondays, as the time difference between New Zealand and the US meant my Monday was their Sunday, and my email would go quiet just long enough to let me breathe.

My new US boss arrived around one year post-acquisition. They were big, bold and ambitious, with a level of assertiveness I had never seen before. They proudly claimed to sleep less than five hours each night. Throughout the group, they were revered for their stamina and their ability to navigate the globe from the comfort of first class without any obvious signs of tiring.

On one particular meeting in the US, they informed me they would be flying to see me in New Zealand just a day after my return. They would arrive on a Sunday, so I asked if they would like me to recommend some options to relax and enjoy the city. They responded emphatically, saying that they expected me to pick them up from their hotel and to be their tour guide for the day. Don't get me wrong, I love playing host to international guests, but I had been away for ten days, and my priority was seeing my children. It was clear I had no option.

The day they arrived I woke up with the flu. I was somewhat relieved – now I could spend the day in bed with my family close by. However, when I called my boss it transpired that the flu was not a reason to cancel a day of sightseeing. So, even though my body was aching and my head throbbing, I was told in no uncertain terms that I was still expected to pick them up, and that they were expecting a full day of tourist highlights. I dragged myself out of bed, dosed to the maximum on painkillers, and put on my best, most hospitable face as I prepared to lead a party of one on a series of photo opportunities across the region.

That's when it got weird.

My boss had purchased a small fox soft toy on their way through transit in some unknown location. They were convinced it was a wombat, a rotund native Australian marsupial that looks nothing like a fox. It is also an animal that has no connection to New Zealand whatsoever, which made my boss's next request even more absurd.

This sly fox became the focal point of my boss's attention as they navigated sightseeing spots around the city. They would prop up the soft toy at every possible chance and have me take a picture of the two of them together. My boss had no children I was aware of to share these photos with, and they gave no explanation of who these photos were for. Their motivation seemed to purely be creating the facade that they were living it up, having a blast in a foreign city. Social media was in its early days – this was well before Instagram or TikTok – but it seemed these photos were so my boss could showcase a dream lifestyle as a jet-setting executive. The illusion they were creating spoke of a bigger issue – one of dominance and control. I knew that they were idolised by investors for the financial returns they were achieving, and they were feared by their colleagues. It was a dangerous combination that was never going to have a fairy-tale ending.

## Diversity is good business

Some people are prepared to take a high-stakes approach to achieving their personal ambitions. The people they meet along the way are mere obstacles on the road to achievement. Highly ambitious organisations gravitate towards these individuals, as they're self-contained, self-motivated and driven to succeed. But, in hiring the human equivalent of a hand grenade, companies fail to recognise that businesses are their own ecosystems, and they can only truly thrive with the right balance of elements. One wrong organism can tip the entire system off balance.

There are also many systemic issues that can disempower employees from being their very best selves. One area ready for disruption is the ranks of executive teams and governance boards. The lack of diversity in both has long been a signal of outdated practice. While the issues of limited cultural and gender diversity are incredibly important, my concern extends to the issue of similarly skilled and qualified people sitting round the board and exec tables, reinforcing each other's ideas.

Almost all sectors recruit people who look, act and respond in similar ways, and this conformity creates significant issues.

Take banking, for example. If you look at the senior executive team of a bank, you'll typically see very limited representation of people who don't have significant experience working in banking and finance. The leader will have spent many years earning their stripes within the banking sector, whether that's in human resources, IT security, customer service or finance. At the top table the chief executive likely has a lifetime of banking experience, and the board of governors will boast an impressive array of financial and banking roles.

If we lived in a world where everything was constant, drawing exclusively from the expertise of people with deep sector knowledge would make total sense. But we don't and it doesn't. When the most strategic roles in an organisation are limited to the pool of people who have deep sector expertise, it hinders the organisation's ability to introduce new ideas and to innovate. The first issue is that the world outside of the sector becomes invisible, as groupthink assumes all things are static. This makes it almost impossible to present new ideas, opportunities and advances, and they are easily dismissed because of a lack of understanding and comprehension. The second issue is that highly skilled, talented people in the lower levels of the organisation who have had careers outside banking are prevented from being able to step up into executive roles. The bubble of corporate alignment reinforces the status quo and becomes an impenetrable forcefield of uniformity. These teams and boards become fixtures that outwardly convey a stereotypical 'type' that excludes much of the population.

Almost every organisation has highly credible people who are a little bit eccentric. It can typically take longer to get to know them, as normal evaluation processes can't put them into boxes. I have grown to love these individuals and their left-of-field thinking. Their view of the world keeps me on my guard, and they also make me feel like I'm missing an important part of life – they seem to understand the inner workings of the world in a way I will never understand.

One such person has worked with me for many years. He has a master's degree in fine arts and a PhD in biochemistry. He was a paediatric oncologist and research fellow at Harvard Medical School and a research fellow at the Malaghan Institute. No one could ever question his intellect or the breadth of his knowledge, however, his communication style is so unpredictable that I have watched people stare wide-eyed in disbelief as he writes pencil notes on his MacBook lid or wanders down the road, swinging his porcelain teacup, to the local cafe for another caffeine hit. He doesn't intend to throw people off guard; he simply is who he is. And his contributions are significant. He brings a perspective that others can't see.

I love that the world is full of people who don't conform, and who are happy staying true to themselves. But few organisations have worked out what an incredible asset people who challenge our norms are, and how much value they bring. Having diversity of thought and original perspectives in your organisation is like being able to look round a curved wall. Nonconformist individuals ask what others don't and question what we assume. They also remind us that, when someone shows up in a way that isn't instantly recognisable as normal practice, we shouldn't dismiss their contribution as being of less value or relevance. The reality couldn't be further from the truth. Brilliant minds are often brilliant because they spend so little time trying to assimilate into popular collectives or schools of thought.

Academics, intellectuals, neurodiverse people and interesting characters are untapped potential in this world. Now more than ever we need diversity if we are truly hoping to solve our problems in the future.

## No future for bullies

I recently met an Indian woman who shared with me her workplace heartache. She had taken on a new leadership role in a new city, hoping to continue the upward trajectory of her career. She had immigrated to New Zealand 14 years ago and since then had worked extremely hard and excelled. Motivated and committed, she worked impossibly long days out of a self-sacrificing dedication to her children. When she left India, she'd had to leave her two children with her parents due to impossible financial demands from an ex-husband, who was blocking her children from joining her in New Zealand. She had left her violent and loveless marriage to create a new beginning that would provide safety and security for her and her children. Over the years, she'd fought the Indian legal system and eventually, through a combination of legal wins and financial commitments, her children were reunited with her in New Zealand and they were able to focus on their future life together.

When we met, she was grappling with her recent decision to change jobs. Her children were both now professionals, they had married wonderful spouses, and her grandchildren were the light of her life. Single and still young enough to throw herself into her career, she'd agreed to move to a new city to take on more responsibility. She'd been quick to accept the promotion, but after 12 weeks in her new role she found her immediate supervisor undermined and controlled her every move. She said he had full control of her diary and he took great pleasure in determining which of her appointments she was approved to attend. In the absence of other colleagues he would raise his voice, undermine her authority and question her capabilities. He became controlling, passive-aggressive and at times threatening as he made it clear he had the power to control her future career. She told me she had begun to record their conversations so she would have evidence of his behaviour, should she ever get the chance to expose his bullying.

As we sat together talking, she shared that she was worried about leaving her job because she didn't know how her supervisor might treat the next person. It struck me how courageous this woman was, preparing to persevere in a role that came with significant stress rather than allow this man to inflict his behaviour on someone else.

She said she had no idea why her supervisor had decided to make her life so miserable. She was a high-performing, hard-working employee, and her work had been recognised regularly. I wanted to help her gain a better understanding of why she was being subjected to this unjustifiable behaviour but there was no obvious explanation. Her boss simply enjoyed power plays and being in control.

Power plays like this are common in work environments. Very few people go through life without at least one significant issue with a colleague. Narcissists exist at all levels of business, and psychopaths do too. But it does seem that the most extreme character flaws are found in those with leadership roles. Perhaps it's the self-belief of these individuals that propels them to the top, or perhaps they are just such competent illusionists that they can role play and manipulate on a level that most cannot see. The smiling assassin, the passive-aggressor, the manipulator who creates a fictional version of how things played out. In most cases we can learn from our experiences with these types, building deeper resilience and an increased wariness of certain characteristics. But whatever it is that drives a person to go out of their way to inflict fear and dominate others, the only way to win is to leave. Whether this means changing roles, moving to a new division or handing in your resignation, you will never resolve the issue by sticking it out. If your employer fails to see such disruptive behaviour, chances are others won't see it either. Life is too short to set out to prove another person's vindictive intent. You win when they can't.

We all respond differently to different types of leadership, but I am yet to see anyone who uses bullying or intimidation techniques make a lasting positive impact. Thankfully there are now more ways to identify and call out rogue leaders. Whistle-blower policies and internal processes to expose bad behaviour are more prevalent than ever before.

I am incredibly encouraged by the next generation of leaders, who are creating new norms of engagement with their teams. They are the first generation to truly embrace flatter structures, agile practices and more distributed workforces, working in the office, at home and remotely. Work culture is becoming more accountable and transparent.

My leadership style has moved on significantly from my earliest days, when I mimicked the tough-talking actions of the leaders of my time. Trust has become integral to high-functioning organisations, and it starts at the top. My earliest teams had hierarchies and complex layers, but these have fundamentally vanished, and I now have interdisciplinary self-forming project teams that create solutions to move projects and initiatives forward. Equity, diversity and many voices at the decision-making table have shown me, again and again, the need for multiple perspectives to enable good business outcomes.

We are imagining a new working future. Teams are increasingly geographically dispersed as more people work from home, and we employ staff in different regions and even different countries. The four-day working week is emerging as a probable solution to the fatigue caused by our always-on world, which has removed the ability to separate work from home. I suspect it will only be a few more years before a four-day working week becomes the norm.

We all face changes that on first reading sound far-fetched or even inconceivable. Your immediate reaction might be to defend what you know and what's familiar. But what if, by defending the status quo, we miss the opportunity to lead positive change? What can we learn from the power plays of the past that held people back, suppressing productivity and job enjoyment? As the job market extends, and a shortage of skilled talent becomes one of the greatest challenges of our time, how can we find the strength and the courage to embrace new and unfamiliar solutions that may feel a little bit unconventional at first?

As I grow older, I'm conscious that I too am at risk of becoming the out-of-touch leader who sometimes held me back in the early part of my career. I hold on tight to the knowledge that I am open to learning and committed to a lifelong journey of adaptation, but I also know that this will require real commitment and ongoing evaluation. Even the most open leader is prone to making mistakes based on long-standing assumptions and behaviours. All leaders need to recognise the subtleties of change and adopt new knowledge into all key roles. As one generation of staff, customers and suppliers hands over to the next, it is our job to find a common language of change and expectation.

Today's customer expects a level of personalisation and choice. We can only achieve this if we understand market shifts in response to new knowledge. I first developed my leadership skills in a world that was male-dominated, analogue, paper-based and measured by the hours of labour, not the outputs of productivity. Adopting new practices is essential if we are to build solutions for the new era.

You likely have your own examples of people who apparently stepped into your world with the explicit intent of creating misery. I know there are more of these people in the road ahead for me. However, I am hopeful that the most valued characteristics of future leaders will be based on merit and commitment, not power. Eventually I hope the stronghold of hierarchy and control will become so devalued and irrelevant that there won't be anywhere for traditional commanding leaders to go.

Until then, I am working hard to bridge the gap by replacing hierarchy and power with a model of trust and collaboration. Many high-impact organisations, ranging from high-growth tech companies and start-ups, to social enterprises and community and grassroot collectives, are opting for the latter. But this is not my only playground. I work with corporations and government agencies too, who often see me as a freethinker, and I share knowledge and data to drive transformation and change. I have learned to become very patient in these spaces. For more than two decades I have persevered and worked to prepare education and skills development for the future, but the same arguments prevail year after year. In some cases I have outpaced my biggest critics, but there are still people in positions of power who are strong in their commitment to hold the future back.

## Bringing about change

There are thousands of highly talented, good people inside corporations who are constrained by what they can't do. These individuals are doing it hard, fighting a constant battle between what's best and what will be approved. They are immersed in outdated systems, where change is glacial and risk evaluation is cautiously managed by teams of analysts and communication specialists. Earlier in my career, I wondered if people worked in these risk-averse environments because they wanted to coast. Did they deliberately choose to work within allowable guidelines instead of fast-moving, progressive industries? Now I understand many people who work in highly regulated organisations do so because they legitimately want to make a positive difference. I chose to influence change and drive progress from outside these systems; others chose to influence from within. Can effective progress be made inside systems built for control? I like to think that with the right people and the right leadership, change is possible anywhere.

The biggest roadblock is retaining the right people in the system long enough without their motivation diminishing.

You might think I disapprove of corporations but this isn't the case. I don't see corporations as being inherently good or bad. Large listed entities are finely tuned machines that rely on repetition and adherence to standards with minimal deviation. Many bring great value and benefits to the world. Some bring access to affordable services. Where there is a market, there will always be someone willing to create and sell. The big question is, how does an organisation go about addressing market needs? In the process of winning, does someone have to lose?

Today we are confronted by the impact of inequality and inequity, and we should all examine what our organisations do in the harsh light of day. Responding to climate change and reducing carbon use should be a required part of a business's licence to operate, but in its absence the voice of public opinion is amplifying.

I don't pass judgement on people who work in industries that have a dubious record. I assume each individual makes their own call on whether the work they do is meaningful. I have friends who've worked for years in organisations that aren't aligned with their personal values. Many have found solace in the organisation's ability to be impactful in other areas, such as sponsorships or employment pathways.

Other friends will only work for companies that have a clear benefit to people and the planet. For them, there is no compromise. How we seek meaning in our work is highly personal and there is no one-size-fits-all when it comes to deriving purpose. I am encouraged by organisations that take a strong stand on values, and those who are guided by a set of principles. More and more businesses are following the process of 'doing good', as business conscience extends beyond philanthropic enterprise to everyday activities.

Driving change from inside or outside any large system requires commitment for the long haul. Moving the dial is hard graft and it can take years or even decades to achieve. Until then it is important not to be dismissive of smaller wins along the way.

One benefit of working at the heart of a system undergoing transformation is that many successes can be achieved by creating momentum and building engagement. More and more young people are comfortable taking their employers to task in areas such as carbon reduction, diversity, leadership accountability and flexible employment agreements.

There is no better example of a global changemaker than Greta Thunberg. She has brought world leaders to the table and asked them to be accountable for their actions, including their lack of decisiveness. She has put parents on notice for not taking responsibility for their children's future. Using internet-based platforms, hard data and a call for action, Greta has become one of the most influential activists of the modern world. Her no-nonsense call out to the citizens of Planet Earth has become a great instrument of climate change debate. All the while Greta has been intentional with her challenge to the older generations pulling the political and economic strings. She has asked them to prioritise the environment over everything else. Her argument is sound, the science is real and yet four years on she is facing the same amplified levels of negativity that she experienced in her earliest protests. What will it take for some people to accept that change is inevitable and that if we do nothing at all we will condemn future generations to an uninhabitable planet? Are we really prepared for what the future holds if we don't change?

I may be called a futurist, a disruptor and a changemaker, but I am driven by a desire to bring about positive change. I use words, data, information and research to show a better way forward.

## It starts with you

Very few New Zealand organisations have team members focused on insights, data and research specific to their sector or any other. Developing strategies and planning for the future requires a deep understanding of the world today and tomorrow. I recommend every business start their strategic planning sessions by listing their assumptions. This might include assumptions on market share, competitors, supply-chain considerations or proven channels to market. Each area should then be tested through research and insights from the global market. New entrants, digital disruptors, new materials, improved or declining logistics channels, new social media and changing demographics are just a few of the considerations that should be taken into account.

Many organisations, from small businesses to large enterprises, spend too little time on culture. Ideally the culture of an organisation should be the topic of regular workshops, where all team members openly share their views and communicate their concerns. Too often sessions on workplace dynamics become presentations on the aspects that are going well, with very little time dedicated to what's not working. Glossing over issues such as biases in hiring, lack of diversity in specific teams, and limited career progression and professional development opportunities means they are left to a couple of people with a very narrow view of the organisation.

If you are in a role or a relationship where the balance of control is dominated by behaviours and actions that are misaligned to your own, or where your contribution isn't acknowledged, it's important to know there are options. There are no prizes for perseverance or for tolerating a situation that makes you feel devalued or demoralised.

Some of the most obvious signs that your organisation (or relationship) is not good for you include:

1. not all input is valued
2. processes or policies are not adhered to equally
3. communication is limited or held back as a means of control
4. leaders show a lack of empathy when you or other members of your team face personal challenges
5. there are closed-door meetings or controlled information flows that only some people have access to
6. privileges are offered to some members of the team but not others.

With every year that passes, we see change occurring as society raises awareness of the flaws and kinks in our business systems. Organisations are facing higher levels of scrutiny and accountability than ever before, and employees hold more power than in any previous era. Often employers address these changing needs only after an internal investigation is launched in response to known issues or injustices. But progress doesn't need to be built off the back of adversity or conflict – it can come through a proactive decision to highlight what needs to be reviewed. A fresh pair of eyes and the power of the collective can be very effective at addressing behaviours that no longer reflect the world we live in. Like many great initiatives that lead to change, it's often best to start with a conversation. Words are louder than actions, even when they don't always fall on receptive ears. It's amazing how many people don't know what they don't know. Calling out what you see might just be the start of a positive change that benefits many.

## CHAPTER 8

# What makes a leader?

Create the future you aspire to have

## All the time in the world

It was July 2016, the middle of winter in Auckland, New Zealand, and I had been invited to a local event to meet the second most powerful man in the world: US Vice President Joe Biden. First, let me set the scene. The invitation had come with very formal instructions about when to arrive, details of the security screening that would be required on entry and a schedule of the proceedings. I was excited to hear Biden speak in person, and the evening before the event I talked with my eldest son about how I would be spending the following evening. I wasn't entirely sure he would even know who the vice president was. After all, he was a teenager and US politics was hardly a topic of everyday conversation for him. It turned out, however, that Biden had a cameo in the US sitcom *Parks and Recreation*, and 'Joe' had become a global pop-culture idol to young people. To my son, Joe was a role model and an icon of the free world.

As soon as I entered the hotel venue it was clear this was not a typical networking event. The walk-through X-ray had been newly installed and my bag was searched. Like many of the people in the room, I had attended global networking events where company presidents and CEOs would take the stage to launch major new products. These so-called town halls were always planned down to the most exacting detail, including the size of the serviettes. Teams of event planners would watch from the wings, just out of view and ready to step in if anything fell out of place. Large corporations use theatre and drama to design their internal events to elicit a specific response. At international shareholder events where dividend returns are well below expected rates, they shun excess and grandstanding in favour of frugality and a sombre mood – the hospitality is simpler and the opulence understated. Good news, new products and increased financial returns, however, are delivered with as much fanfare as can be squeezed into a 90-minute experience.

So there I was, at a hotel about to meet the Vice President of the United States. The event was warming up and the volume of chatter in the room was increasing as the champagne flowed. The stage in front of the room was roped off in celebratory red-blue-and-white-striped rope between gold bollards. An enormous US flag hung at the back of the makeshift stage and stunning flower arrangements marked the perimeter.

Right on cue, we were told to hush as the vice president took the stage. He entered with a spring in his step, wearing the smile that has now become his globally recognised trademark. His presence filled the entire room. Everyone was quiet. We held on to his words as they passed from him to us; he was captivating, sincere and humble.

It was right about this time that I was tapped on the back and asked if I would like to join a small group of people to have a private meet and greet with the vice president. We would be escorted to a different room in the hotel, where Biden would mix with us over a glass of wine. Though absolutely disbelieving, I confirmed I'd be delighted to accept this opportunity.

Being 'escorted' in this specific situation meant each invited guest was matched with just one other, and in pairs we were led to a hotel lift flanked by two security men dressed in US military uniforms. We rapidly exited the lift a few floors later and crossed to another lift in order to disguise our final destination to anyone observing from the ground floor. It felt very cloak-and-dagger as we entered a beautifully laid out private room where around a dozen fellow business people gathered.

I knew most of the guests, and we all looked somewhat dazed by the unlikelihood of the situation but incredibly excited by the opportunity. I glanced around the room and realised there were about the same number of US security personnel as there were guests. They meant business, standing tall with straight backs and expressions that gave nothing away. It wasn't long before Biden entered the room and he stopped to talk to each of us one by one. He referred to all of us by name, as supplied by our name badges, and made eye contact for the full duration of each personal conversation. I was one of the last guests he spoke to, and, as with others in the group, he shook my hand then cupped it, signalling that I had his full attention. He looked me in the eyes and simply said, 'Tell me about Frances Valintine.'

Our interaction was reminiscent of a conversation with a warm-hearted family member who is interested in filling in the gaps since you last saw them. There was no sense that he had other priorities to attend to, no sign that he wanted to be anywhere else but there in that room, chatting with a group of strangers late on a winter's night.

As he turned to leave, he gave me one last smile and I thought of my son and what he would've done to be where I was standing. As a closing remark, I told Biden that my son was a huge fan and said that he would be thrilled that I'd met him in person. Without dropping a beat he asked for my son's name and his age. I said he was an 18-year-old student. Biden asked if I had my phone, which I promptly pulled from my handbag. He then asked me to call my son and pass the phone to him.

This was when my heart started to beat like a jackhammer in my chest. I dialled my son's number, handed the phone over and quietly crossed my fingers in hope that my son would answer the phone, and that he would answer in a style appropriate for a vice president.

It turned out my son did answer. Politely. My heart slowed as I watched one side of the conversation. They chatted about studies, life and interests. The security personnel around the room all leaned in, trying to eavesdrop, their faces now ominous frowns of controlled concern. After all, this was an uncleared phone call to an unknown person who was busy chatting away to the vice president as though they were two friends idly passing time.

This experience was as profound at the time as it seems to me now, six years later. The vice president is now the president, but I suspect if the same small group event played out today, the outcome would be the same.

The call to my son and the way Biden worked his way around the room was one of the most extraordinary displays of leadership I have ever seen. There was no ego. Every person in that small hotel meeting room was treated in exactly the same way, regardless of who they were or what they did, including the staff serving refreshments.

I have worked with many different leaders in my life and one of the less desirable traits I have witnessed is impatience. This character flaw often plays out when it's obvious the leader is looking beyond the person they're talking to, seeking out more influential connections. In a world that demands more and more of our attention, and as connectivity creeps from our offices into our homes, it's important that we all take note of how we show up. It is not just the first impression that lasts, but every one that follows.

This is not as straightforward as it sounds. I constantly battle my diary and the relentless bombardment of meetings and calls. I have days and weeks when I look back and think about the way I interacted with people around me, knowing there have been plenty of times when tiredness, work pressure and life distractions prevented me from being fully present. In these moments I think back to Joe Biden. The demands on his time are enormous. The decisions he makes don't just affect a few people, they affect hundreds of thousands, even millions, and yet in that room he appeared to have limitless availability. He changed the life of my son that day, but he changed my life too. There are many leadership characteristics that define success, but none are more important than the ability to listen and to arrive in every situation checked in and present.

## The great equaliser

Leading and making meaningful progress in life and work comes with both rewards and challenges. For me the hardest part of fronting a movement of progress was the need to spend so much time offshore when my children were young. I chose to have children while still in my late twenties, a decision I am incredibly thankful for now that I get to spend time with them as adults. They bring me so much love and joy. But this doesn't take away from my regret that, as they entered primary school, my career was on an upward trajectory. I had significant responsibilities and much of my time was spent on planes and at meetings in boardrooms offshore. Strangely, even though this was not that long ago, technology has now removed the need to spend so much time flying to visit clients or make deals over shared tables. The exponential adoption rate of video conferencing is probably one of the greatest benefits of two years of rolling lockdowns.

But in the 2000s attending events across the world was an essential part of running a business and building a network of diverse friends and colleagues. The more globally connected the business, the more events and international meetings you were expected to attend.

One corporate retreat stands out from all the others. It was a gathering of global presidents who worked for a US company that had acquired Media Design School. The retreat was designed to bring all the regional leaders together in a remote venue, where our strategic priorities would be shared and aligned with the overarching strategic priorities of the company. As the CEO of Media Design School, I was one of the regional presidents. The term president felt so grandiose to me sitting in my office in Auckland city, where status was downplayed. My business card simply said CEO but, in this setting, we were all presidents and vice presidents.

This gathering of the minds took place in Aspen, Colorado, at a venue frequented by wealthy skiers and golfers. I had flown into Aspen from Auckland off the back of a 24-hour flight across the South Pacific. When I arrived at my villa, I found instructions asking me to join my international colleagues at an evening barbecue that had already started.

I was relatively new to the company and my induction had been limited to a few short phone and Skype calls, where names and faces hadn't fully connected in my mind. With no indication of the dress code for the barbecue, I faced a wardrobe dilemma. Would this be a casual event or one where I was expected to dress formally? I decided to hedge my bets and err on the side of caution, and opted for a summer dress paired with open-toed sandals. As I walked down the steps to the gathering, I was astounded to see all the men dressed in suits with open-necked shirts and all the women in block-colour cocktail dresses, even though it was a Sunday evening in the vast wilderness of the Rocky Mountains. My inexperience with global corporate retreats meant I had wrongly assumed that at a barbecue I could break the unwritten rule of conformity. There was a corporate uniform that kept everyone within a common range of behaviour and said, 'I belong.'

My overriding desire was to do a U-turn and head back to my room to change into a more appropriate dress, but I was too far into the room to retreat. I put on a smile and carried on walking. I wondered how many people attending this international gathering wished they could put on a pair of shorts and a casual shirt on that hot summer evening. Or had everyone become so institutionalised that no one gave it a second thought?

Adhering to conformity has never been one of my strongest attributes, and in settings where individualism is seen as noncompliance, I often find myself playing a game of snap in my head, matching people wearing the same shoes or the same striped blue shirt. With all the options and colours in the rainbow, how did dress codes like khaki chinos for casual outings become the sign of belonging?

I observed the power plays taking place around the room and immediately sensed that trust could not be taken for granted. For all intents and purposes, we were all colleagues working for the same company in different corners of the world. But an invisible leader board was sitting above everyone's head, as the financial performance of our respective organisations was compared and judged. We were there to showcase our successes and find ways to play down our losses. I had written my financial presentation weeks before, and it had been analysed, scrutinised and edited dozens of times by members of the US finance team, who were adamant that the only story to tell was one of endless success. This was not the time to share learnings or talk about projects that weren't doing so well.

These financial sessions dedicated to creating impressive reports were the first time I saw the amount of manipulation that goes into the facade of endless success. I realised that I didn't have it in me to lead a business solely motivated by financial returns, or one that needed smoke and mirrors. I just didn't have the stomach to put profit over people. Equality, fairness and trust are not words that sit easily in the world of managed funds and investment. It turns out I am not the only one who experiences this dilemma. In hundreds of conversations I've spoken to many graduate students who are planning their exit from a role that is misaligned with their core values. Working in a sector where you must manipulate data to reduce tax or impress shareholders may be entirely legal, but it doesn't suit everyone.

I was learning that I was not alone in my discomfort with the 'at all costs' culture. The turnover of staff at these gatherings was more like a gym membership than a highly functional global executive team. Every six weeks we'd meet in another part of the world and a group of newly minted executives would turn up, replacing those who had simply disappeared. A limited pool of people demonstrate the very unique set of skills to thrive in organisations that are bound by the need for endless returns. I can now identify these particular characteristics from afar – the type of person driven by money and the challenge of going in for the win. I can't help but wonder what defines their world beyond the endless pursuit of power. With no other working environment to compare it to, do people assume all companies operate by the same rules?

The Aspen executive retreat provided further validation that I was a square peg in a round hole, but it was memorable for another reason too. The day after the barbecue we were all sitting in a large conference room with tables and chairs laid out in a U shape, with the most senior leaders and the global president sitting in the centre of the curve. We were looking at financial slides projected on to a screen on the far wall. The door nearest the head of the table had been left open to allow the Colorado summer breeze to circulate. The mood was serious, and, with the exception of the person presenting, there wasn't a murmur to be heard.

I was sitting between two colleagues from Israel and Italy when a loud shriek filled the room. There, diagonally across from where I sat, a mid-sized black bear walked in.

If it hadn't been a potentially serious situation, it would've actually been very funny. I watched in awe as my super-fit Israeli colleague immediately leaped out of her chair and literally rolled across the floor towards the exit closest to where we sat. She had disappeared before the rest of us had even registered what was happening. Fortunately, with the ruckus of furniture being rapidly pushed back and the cacophony of shouts, the bear simply turned and vacated the room, heading back into the undergrowth.

I have been fortunate enough to have hiked in many places where wildlife and people happily coexist, including deep in the Costa Rican rainforest and in the Bornean wilderness. In these cases I travelled knowing and planning for the possibility that a wild animal might cross paths with me. In this specific instance, however, the bear simply showed up in our conference room to remind us who the boss really was. Even the most beautifully executed display of financial reporting didn't stop nature from having the last laugh.

The behaviour that'd played out in the few seconds after the bear entered the room taught me a lot about power. In that moment of chaos, there was no hierarchy, no ability to claim greater importance and no unfair advantage from having schmoozed the global president. The natural world was the great equaliser, reminding us that we were merely a random group of humans in a room, stressing over profit margins.

When I think back to that conference room in Aspen when the bear strolled in, I can still recall how each of my international colleagues reacted. At that moment, each individual's true colours, their real self, shone through. Minutes earlier they had all been playing the corporate game, but in that moment of bear-induced madness we were stripped of titles, experience and hierarchy – all that was left was our raw reactions. Not all of it was pretty. There was plenty of shoving and pushing as instinct took over. The fight-or-flight response went into overdrive and nobody fought or took a protective stance for others. The battle to get out of the room was survival of the fittest.

Within three years of this event, I decided it was time to leave. The expected compromises to meet shareholder demands were misaligned with my own values. Thankfully I had trusted people around me, who reminded me that my ideas were not too big, too audacious or too future-focused – I just needed the ability to develop them outside the corporate system.

## People watching

Over the years I have learned to have fully functioning conversations while my other senses focus on what people's non-verbal reactions are saying. Sensing and translating what words don't say has become one of my most highly tuned skills. I particularly use it when hiring new team members. Even if I'm not in the interview, I will often observe an applicant's body language and how they're engaging with staff. First interviews are generally held in open areas of our offices, where there are people moving around and engagement opportunities can form naturally. Given my mantra that new staff be open and willing to learn, I am very mindful of how people will fit into the culture of the organisation. All new staff members must show they will connect with the people around them, regardless of ethnicity, age or role.

We all have this superpower. First impressions really do count. For me, the 'don't hire dickheads' rule counts for everyone. If I end up stranded on an island with my team, I want to know that everyone will play nicely. Work takes up too much time in our lives to deal with people who are judgemental or unwilling to support others to grow and develop.

My fascination with people watching started early in life. I travelled to countries with unfamiliar languages at a time when communicating through a mix of sign language and pocket-sized translation books was standard practice. One particular unplanned excursion, to the Greek island of Cos, gave me a front-row seat in learning to talk through gestures.

I had headed across the Aegean Sea between Turkey and Cos to have my Turkish visa renewed. The weather turned stormy and strong crosswinds prevented my ferry home from docking in the harbour. A 12-hour Greek island stay turned into a five-day Greek island stay, as I hunkered down in the only local pub that stayed open in the winter. The small, single bedroom where I stayed was intended for staff, and it had a wardrobe where brooms were stored. Day and night the sound of Greek music would carry through the floorboards, filling my small space with the sounds of an unfamiliar language. For four of the five days, I sat at a table in the bar sheltering from the weather that thrashed around outside. I watched the same small group of elderly men drinking ouzo, a local anise-flavoured aperitif, sharing stories and laughing. Over these four days I learned about the lives of these men, their relationship to one another and the bond that they held. Even with an unfamiliar language you can't camouflage key attributes of a person's character. Good people are good people in any language. Body language tells the story of generosity in the same way that people who are self-indulgent, arrogant or selfish don't need to speak to be clearly understood.

According to Albert Mehrabian, Professor Emeritus of Psychology at the University of California, Los Angeles, the way we communicate follows a 7–38–55 rule: words account for only

7 per cent of the overall message we hear, tone of voice accounts for 38 per cent, and the remaining 55 per cent is communicated by our body language. Most of us spend very little time thinking about how we come across in the moment we first meet someone, or what our body language says about our willingness to be there. In many aspects of working life we rely too greatly on autopilot, without paying conscious attention to what makes us truly happy.

## An active state of mind

Leadership and leading change requires an active state of mind. We are what we imagine. We can change the trajectory of our future if we focus on what we're passionate about, and where our talents and skills are best used. Knowing your skills and talent are being underutilised can be the most demoralising way to live. Conversely, contributing, being valued and feeling that your contribution makes a difference is far more valuable than any pay cheque – even if it means you have to take a lower-paying role or start your own venture. If you're looking to find the confidence to take on a new role, head in a new direction or step outside your comfort zone, know that we all have it within us to create the future we aspire to.

Great leaders feel strongly about what they do. They focus on opportunities, not obstacles, and they are purposeful about what they spend their time on. We all admire people for different reasons. Leadership is not limited to those at the top of the pyramid in large organisations; people who bring communities together and lead change initiatives that benefit others are also leaders. Building trust and leading by example are core to propelling your life and career forward. There are no backseat roles if you want to make a difference. Living is a full-participation role that invites you to make a difference.

## CHAPTER 9

# Starting a new chapter

## Get going

### Visualising the road ahead

It's 2011 and I'm in the home of my US boss, watching the smoke from the candles on my fortieth birthday cake waft across the room. Coincidentally one of my colleagues is also turning 40 today, so there are two birthday cakes on the table. He's from Switzerland, but in many ways our journeys are similar. Being born on the same day in the same year ties us to many of the same events and influences, regardless of where we grew up. There is something weirdly reassuring about knowing someone who has had the same number of days on the planet as me.

The scientific odds of a specific thing happening are fascinating. The well-documented birthday paradox states that in a room of just 23 people, there's a 50:50 chance at least two of them have the same birthday. In a room of 75 people, there's a 99 per cent chance at least two people have the same birthday. How is this possible with 365 days in the year? Paradoxes defy intuition, but

I love that sometimes in life, as in business, there isn't an easy explanation as to why some things work out the way they do.

Things happening unexpectedly is part of life, but we still assume each day is predictable. Most days do follow the entries on the calendars beaming out from our smartphones. We humans are bold – we like to plan and make decisions for the future, even though we know unexpected events can turn an ordinary day into a day we'll remember for the rest of our lives.

Birthdays are often memorable for the collection of friends and loved ones. But not all birthdays are equal. Sometimes our special events are marked by actions outside of our control – the clash with another big event, a Covid lockdown, an unexpected weather event or an unfortunately timed illness.

But on my fortieth birthday, as I stand in a dining room in Aspen, I make a commitment to myself to start a master's degree.

In hindsight, I'm not sure I had really thought through the logistics. I would somehow need to balance study with a week overseas each month as the CEO of Media Design School. Even more questionable was my decision to study a residential programme in Melbourne, meaning even more time on planes and in hotels.

My study focused on the emergence of online learning in the days before Zoom was the norm. Alongside my master's, I continued to work across three continents, flying back and forth to board meetings and driving projects to grow the global business I was leading.

As I entered my forties, I decided that I would start a new business that would keep me away from airports and all-night board meetings. I knew my passion and talent for technology and education would be at the heart of my new venture. What I didn't know was how far away from my career trajectory I would step, pursuing and creating a venture designed to teach children.

I had no educational background in teaching children. My entire career history had been focused on higher education, technology and the teaching of adults. I also knew nothing about the formal school curriculum. What I did know was from my own children's learning and their school experience. This insight was enough for me to recognise that their education looked too similar to my own decades earlier, even though everything had changed and their futures and careers would look very different from my own.

## Building a learning environment fit for the future

In my 14 years at Media Design School, from 1999 to 2013, I was immersed in the development of adults learning advanced coding, film animation and game development. I watched as adult students closed the door on one chapter of their lives to open up another. They were pivoting away from the traditional creative industries to embrace the new technologies of the time. But during the same period my own children did not have a single element of technology in their schooling. By 2012 my oldest son was 14, and, as I watched him pack his backpack with textbooks each day before heading to school, I wondered how his generation would adapt to an increasingly digital world if they knew nothing about it. I was concerned that my children were missing out and I could see the signals of digital adoption in the marketplace, so I left my CEO role. The creation of The Mind Lab had begun.

By mid-2013 I was in a factory in China learning about robots. This wasn't any robot factory – it was owned by a company focused on developing and designing robots to teach young children how to program robots through scripted commands using a simple graphical user interface (GUI). From there I travelled to Europe and Scandinavia to find out how children there were being introduced to technology in open, non-prescriptive learning environments, where play-based learning formed the building blocks of creativity and innovation. In particular, I focused on the Finnish education system, which was grounded in creativity, active play and support.

I'll resist taking you down the rabbit hole of the many, many limitations of the industrial model of education that still dominates the way children learn. Everyone has a view on education and, depending on how the school system served or failed you, these views can be very different. My greatest dream is for the New Zealand education system to be more responsive to and proactive about changing needs. I'll continue to chip away at the edges, knowing there are many obstacles ahead. Even with a lifetime of effort I may never see education fully contextualised in the world our children see outside the classroom.

Challenging the stronghold of traditional education is not for the faint-hearted. I decided to build an organisation committed to teaching digital technology and creativity to children, and in doing so I learned more about human behaviour than I had in my entire career teaching adults. In the very first classes, teaching 7-year-olds to 12-year-olds, my team and I soon learned that parents and teachers who visited The Mind Lab with their children fell into one of four categories.

The first group were easy to identify: the helicopter parents who literally could not extract themselves from beside their children. They were so concerned about their children's success that their physical presence was a literal backup drive, ensuring that if the child missed anything, the parent would be there to put them back on track.

Parents or teachers who were deeply troubled by the lack of formal instruction made up the second group. They would watch, concerned, as their children and students pondered how to make a code work, or how to solve a challenge, working together and learning by doing. They would often murmur in hushed tones about the absence of worksheets or instruction manuals. These new ways of teaching were so different from what they were familiar with.

The third group gave very little thought to how their children learned. They were parents and teachers who entrusted education to others. They weren't uninterested in their children, but they had little real interest in the process of learning. Conversations about cognitive development, different ways of learning or the development of neural networks were lost on them. They were happy to outsource the responsibility of learning to others, often including tutors in after-school sessions.

The parents of creative kids, bright kids, kids with ADHD and autism, and highly imaginative kids fell into a fourth group. They were animated in their praise for their children and constructive in their feedback. They were happy to watch on as their children explored, imagined, tested and theorised different ideas and concepts. This group of kids and their parents were all the motivation I ever needed to keep going. Our entire team of creatives, scientists, inventors, coders and tinkerers loved these kids. We could all see our younger selves in these enthusiastic minds, thinking only of possibility and potential – no rules or instructions needed.

Before long, our single education lab turned into two, then three and then four. Each day hundreds of school children across the country would arrive in school buses and vans at our labs, where they would spend a few hours immersed in the technology of their time. Robotics, 3D printing, 3D modelling, coding and development replaced traditional books, and the creative outputs were exciting, original and profound.

These learning labs were noisy and filled with activity and the hum of excitement. I observed in absolute awe as many small hands created stop-motion films, or as the children organised themselves into teams to build robots that they then programmed to undertake tasks and follow instructions, before chasing these programmed robots around the lab. There was an electrifying audioscape of mass productivity and innovation. It was chaotic, fast-paced and energetic.

There was no blueprint for this type of learning environment. The first lab was located in an ex-warehouse that was colourful, quirky and creative. I loved watching as children looked around and experienced learning through a different lens. The students loved stepping up to the responsibility of trying out new technologies and doing things they thought of as strictly for adults, like coding websites or building augmented-reality experiences.

## New heights

I was so busy trying to keep the doors open on my resource-intensive business that I stopped noticing what was going on outside the labs. My team was growing rapidly and we were spending so much time brainstorming new and exciting ways to challenge the children that I missed a market shift that was beginning to take place. Parents were noticing, schools were noticing and the topic of education was changing. These were early days but already tens of thousands of children had experienced a session in one of our labs and the conversation about digitisation in education was becoming louder. Quiet, more reserved students were stepping forward to lead initiatives. Kids who often found learning challenging were problem-solving and sharing their ideas excitedly with others. Teachers were astounded. In the labs the energy was soaring. Children as young as five were coding. Some older children were working together to develop computer games, others were modelling 3D replicas of 2D images for printing on the 3D printer.

In July 2014, less than one year after opening my first learning lab for children, I found myself at the Talent Unleashed Awards as a finalist for our work at the lab. I had no idea who had nominated me or how they knew about the work we were doing, but I was quietly thrilled that our work was being recognised, even if only by a single nominating supporter.

The event was like no other awards function I have ever attended. It was broadcast simultaneously in three time zones and four different countries – live and online. In a pre-Zoom world of slow VDSL internet connectivity, this was quite an ambitious undertaking.

Local events were being held across the Asia Pacific region, where local finalists selected for their commitment to leading change initiatives competed for regional recognition. Given New Zealand's lead in the global-time-zones race, our event started first, followed by Australia, Singapore and Hong Kong.

Given the newness of my venture, I had little expectation of winning. I attended mostly out of interest to see what other organisations were doing in the impact space. When the New Zealand award winner was announced, I was truly astounded to hear the name of my organisation being read by the host. This surprise was soon surpassed a couple of hours later, when the overall winner for Asia Pacific was announced by Sir Richard Branson, who was beaming in from Sydney. My name was called and I was invited to the stage to accept the award. Richard Branson's announcement was being broadcast simultaneously across four countries, and I just sat there at my table, looking at the screen. I knew on some level of consciousness that my name had been announced but for some reason my brain just didn't compute. I sat there until my friend literally poked me in the ribs to jostle me into reality and nudge me towards the stage.

While my exchange with Richard Branson was only a virtual interaction across thousands of kilometres of ocean, my rendition of a deer in headlights was just as real as if he'd been in the room. But Sir Richard didn't have the stage all to himself – he was joined online by one of my all-time technology gurus, Steve Wozniak, the co-founder of Apple. I had followed every step of Steve's journey as Apple iPods, iPhones and iPads came to dominate the world. I had been a fan since the first Power Mac G4 in 1999, when

Apple was tracking towards becoming the largest publicly traded corporation in the world.

The importance of the award was far bigger than what it seemed on paper and in the press. I was nearly a year into one of the most challenging business start-ups of my life, and I was running low on sleep and inspiration. A government-owned organisation had recently invested in the business, and already there were two distinctly different ideologies and conflicting priorities at play. On top of this, my master's papers were backing up and my thesis submission date was drawing closer. The recognition of the award gave me an injection of confidence and renewed hope, justifying all the hard work and long days, and receiving it from two of the most famous business idols in the world gave the entire team a massive boost. We tightened our belts and dug in with a renewed sense of commitment to break through the barriers of change. I found myself working even harder to facilitate conversations that would shift resistance in education. I found a new voice and built up the confidence to step into the legacy spaces of education that were the hardest to move. I identified influential people who supported my cause for change, and who could help me remove the barriers of outdated practices and views.

The prize for winning the award was the opportunity to spend time at the Branson School of Entrepreneurship in Johannesburg, South Africa. It aimed to connect me with other global entrepreneurs and promised time with Richard Branson himself. But I never got to experience this opportunity – it was to be the start of a series of failed interactions with Richard Branson. Two unfortunately scheduled meetings prevented me from spending time with one of the world's most iconic entrepreneurs.

However, I did end up sharing the stage with Steve Wozniak a few years later, when we co-judged the Talent Unleashed Awards in Sydney. We interviewed the award finalists live on stage, and he was funny, engaging and incredibly skilled at cutting to the chase. I was in awe.

Everyone has their idols, the people we watch from afar and admire as they carry out their everyday activities. I have music heroes and actor crushes, but I have always admired people who develop ideas into impactful businesses. The idea of coming up with a problem to solve and turning it into something of value and significance is fascinating to me. That said, motivations vary greatly from person to person, and I have discovered this can be confronting as each person has their own values and ethics. How someone uses their time or makes business decisions often comes down to their moral compass and priorities.

With a significant award in hand and newfound mojo, I upped the ante. In August 2014 I took on yet another challenge, developing the digital skills and knowledge of teachers, who are at the frontline of change. They face a new generation of students who have only ever known the internet and who are increasingly challenging the logic of what they're taught and how they're taught it.

I was on a roll. The most challenging financial concerns of the first year of trade were almost behind me. I had a financial partner, my master's thesis was all but written, and I was spending more time than ever with my children.

## Best laid plans

With the promise of smooth sailing in sight, everything changed. My 14-year-old son had a growth on his neck. After a series of blood tests, we were asked to head to the oncology ward at the children's hospital for a biopsy to be taken. We were reassured that this was precautionary as teenagers often have inflamed lymph nodes. They told me I shouldn't worry and that it would take at least three days to get the results back. They would invite my son and me to come back into hospital for the results as standard procedure, so reassured me not to be worried when they called us back in.

I was scheduled to be a keynote speaker at an event in another city the day after my son's biopsy. All I wanted to do was to stay close to my son, but there was nothing I could do but wait. I decided to proceed with my speaking commitment as the anguish of waiting quietly for his results was unbearable.

With a heavy heart, I flew to the city where my speaking gig was being held. I switched on my mobile phone when I landed, and a call rang through immediately. I didn't recognise the number. It was the oncologist. He was phoning to inform me that my son had stage-four cancer and he would need to be admitted to hospital the next day. My brain shut down. I walked into the airport terminal and recall someone had my name on a card. I know we drove to the conference venue, and I spoke calmly with the technicians at the back of the room about connecting my laptop to their projection system. I remember the room was empty and the only real light came from the illuminated screen at the front. I went to the front row and sat down. I looked at the empty screen, trying to find some space to clear the thoughts that weighed heavy in my mind. I don't know how long I sat there. Eventually I became aware I was not alone. A woman had come over and sat beside me. She introduced herself and told me we'd met before at a business lunch. I looked at her. No words formed.

'Are you OK?' she asked.

I closed my eyes and the tears welled up. I fought them back and tried desperately to form words. Putting her arm round me, she said, 'I don't know what has happened, but if you need me to cover for you I will find something to talk about.'

I looked at her and managed to whisper, 'I just found out my son has cancer.'

She hugged me tight and told me she had my back.

The room behind me had filled and the attendees were waiting for me to take the stage. I walked to the podium and looked out at the waiting crowd. I honestly don't recall what I said, or even whether I was coherent. My body and mind were having a circuit failure. I tried to focus on delivering my talk, but questions kept forming in my head. It all feels hazy now.

At some point I cut my talk off. The woman who had spoken to me walked up to the stage and I exited the building into a waiting taxi and headed back to the airport.

To this day I don't know what happened after I walked out. I imagine the woman chatted to the crowd, perhaps sharing an apology from me. Maybe she initiated an impromptu conversation from the floor. I have tried to remember her name so I can thank her, but my brain cells can't join up all the dots. All I know is that on that day she was an angel. My life, it turns out, has had many.

Life throws up so many unexpected challenges. Without a road map to follow or an instruction guide to outline each step, we are at the mercy of a labyrinth of interconnecting forces. We often admire people because of their profile, their great achievements and their highly publicised successes. I have learned that the real heroes are often the people who say very few words, who are strong when you can't be. Having a child with cancer or any life-threatening illness is an experience too many parents face. Nothing can prepare you.

The older we get, the more often we are confronted with the people we care about facing life-threatening illness. It changes your perspective in a nanosecond. Our priorities are very different when unexpected situations make our choices for us. Sometimes this means just putting down your tools to look after your own health or the health of a loved one. Life is too short under the very best of circumstances. I hope no one finds themselves wishing they'd made better choices while they still could.

## CHAPTER 10

# When life takes a U-turn

## Adapt, adapt and adapt again

### Facing down an uncertain future

It is late 2014 and I'm in the local children's hospital, sitting in a waiting room dedicated to teenagers with cancer. I'm not the only parent. We all have the same fixed expressions and the same need to fill the void with polite conversation. We all know each other's circumstances. We know which children have been in and out of this ward for years and which children, like my son, are just starting their treatment. The children themselves are endlessly tested and connected to machines that administer a concoction of chemotherapies. Sometimes the room is empty, and my son and I just talk. We find things of interest that are far removed from the subject of cancer.

Overnight, my world has gone from being global to hyperlocal. I find myself noticing a new series of coincidences as hospital treatments and check-ups fill the weeks in my calendar. My one-year-old start-up business could have been located anywhere in the city, but it's not – it's located in the commercial building closest to the children's hospital. It's a short stroll from my work to the children's cancer ward. My laptop becomes my office and the chair beside the hospital bed becomes my makeshift desk. I feel immensely privileged when I speak with parents and children who travel hours by car or plane just to attend a chemo appointment.

This isn't our only luck. I have lived rurally most of my life, aside from a few stints living in some of the world's most populated cities. I have always been most comfortable surrounded by space, hills, trees, mountains and water. But, whether good luck or good planning, we have recently moved house to be closer to my new business, so my daily commute has shrunk from hours in traffic to a short drive, from home to work to the hospital.

Coincidences are never able to be explained, but it feels like my subconscious has been planning for the events of 2014 before I knew my life was about to change.

When I think back to this time, I instantly recall the heavy emotional toll it took on my entire family. Anyone who has spent time caring for a loved one while they go through treatment or trauma will be familiar with the helplessness and distress you feel in not being able to take away their pain. My son showed the most incredible courage and resilience, and not once did he complain, even as his head was shaved and food lost all appeal.

Sitting alongside my son in the children's hospital, I am surrounded by parents and grandparents carrying the same heavy weight of worry. My son should be enjoying his mid-teens, discovering new interests, playing sports and pushing boundaries, but instead he is watching chemicals pump into his body through a portacath that has been surgically inserted under the skin on his chest.

When your life changes overnight, your sense of time changes too. You move into a mode of slow, slow, fast, depending on what the day brings: periods at the hospital are slow and procedural;

periods between scans and results play out in slow motion; the moments of laughter and joy when my son momentarily forgets his illness are short and pass too quickly.

Eventually the balance will change, and the periods of happiness will extend and outweigh the moments of anguish. Harmony and a sense of calm will return, and my son will once again be his fun-loving self.

Eight years on, I still remember 2014 with the same heaviness that so many across the world felt in 2020 when Covid-19 took hold and pitched the world into an uncertain future. My heart was heavy for very different reasons in 2014 and 2020, but both times my life was turned on its head by an unfamiliar situation with no obvious way through. Normal everyday routines and systems came to a grinding halt and each day delivered a wide range of emotions.

The earliest reports of Covid-19 felt very distant in my world. Every previous high-risk virus had been contained by an imaginary geographic border. To me, it was as though earlier viruses had respected the boundaries of countries, and my awareness of them had solely been through stories in the media. I had sympathised with the images I saw shared in newsfeeds, but the context was so unfamiliar. I couldn't relate it to my everyday reality. By February 2020, as Wuhan went into lockdown and as the virus was first being discovered in other countries, it was soon apparent this was different: Covid-19 was hostile, fast-moving and destructive.

The turmoil unfolded in front of our eyes. Significant anomalies in global datasets started to emerge, and infographics showing the virus's spread made clear it would have far-reaching effects on global health systems. New hospitals were constructed, global demand for hand sanitiser spiked, and panic buying of essentials in stores across the globe set in. Even in those early days when we tried to imagine the worst, we had no idea what would unfold over the following months and years.

As local news coverage reported on the global risks, I was invited to join a national group of business leaders sharing data and scientific information on an online channel, where everyone was expressing concern about what was unfolding. Responses and information flooded in, outlining the urgent mitigations needed to halt transmission. The need to close the borders and quarantine international arrivals quickly went from a quiet murmur to a deafening call for urgent action. No one knew what the right response was, or how the coming weeks and months would turn out, but the growing sentiment was that the border was our frontline of defence. New Zealand prepped for impact, and the headlines turned from the international impact of Covid-19 to our own emerging risks. The agendas at board meetings changed in focus from normal strategic priorities to the business response to Covid-19.

Every business owner has a story of the moment they had to bring their staff together to inform them that the future was looking uncertain. One saving grace was that no one person knew any more about the risk than the next, so the impact of the lockdown and closed borders was playing out in real time for everyone. We tolerated the somewhat hazy decision-making processes based on best-guess assumptions of scientists, statisticians, virologists and health professionals, and the apparent absence of hierarchy and power led to high levels of trust and compliance from the community. As a country, we agreed to follow the rules to keep as many people as possible out of harm's way.

At work I made the announcement that a lockdown was imminent and asked all staff to clear their desks and take everything they needed to work from home. Desk chairs, laptops and monitors were loaded on to trolleys and wheeled out of the building. It was still a few days before the official announcement was made, but the rapid spread of Covid-19 was evident. Our business moved online and, as we tested the robustness of communication channels between staff, partners, clients and students, I was distracted by another pressing development.

The week before we'd packed up boxes to take our work home, I had gone to a commercial property auction where the building we occupied was being sold. The business had grown a lot over the previous two years, and we were operating over two separate buildings located 400 metres apart. The auction took place just two weeks before the first reported case of Covid-19 in New Zealand – the same day that the World Health Organization announced Covid-19 as a global pandemic. I held my breath as my building went under the hammer, hoping the market hadn't been spooked by looming uncertainty. I had already signed a lease agreement for another commercial property just down the road, and if my business was hit badly by the lockdown I would be responsible for a third lease that needed to be paid.

Thankfully the property sold, and my team and I celebrated, imagining the start of a new chapter when we'd all be working under one roof again. It was a poignant moment, signalling the end of our phase as a start-up enterprise and our transition into a substantial organisation.

Twelve days later, as more Covid-19 cases began to emerge around the country, the New Zealand government announced we would go into full lockdown in 48 hours, on 25 March. Everyone would be isolated at home, the only exceptions frontline workers in our hospitals and essential-service operators. As this update played out across the media, it dawned on me that my commercial building would legally settle during the planned lockdown. I had just two days to sort, pack and ship my entire business out of the building, and to locate a carrier who could transport all our furniture to a yet-to-be-determined location.

In these moments you realise how much the team around you can be like family. Everyone was facing the fear of uncertainty and a looming lockdown deadline, but a few of my colleagues still stepped back into the office to help project manage the impossible. It was a frenzy of boxes being assembled, items wrapped and assets ticked off. A freight company that'd had all their future bookings cancelled agreed to pick up our items in a race against the clock. Our new landlords agreed to let us drop all our furniture at the new location, which was still under construction. As the sky darkened, and just hours before the clocks turned to midnight on 25 March 2020, we stacked the last box in place, sanitised our hands and headed to our lockdown locations.

No one imagined that this would be the new normal of business and work for more than a few weeks. If someone had told me that two years later the world would have many millions of deaths and hundreds of millions of Covid-19 cases, it would've been incomprehensible to me. Almost every aspect of business has changed since early 2020. The way we work, live, learn, eat, travel, buy and sell has changed significantly as we've adapted and tried to survive.

The years I've spent working with professionals across multiple sectors has, for me, validated the research on how adults respond to life-changing situations. In the face of unexpected change, regardless of the contributing factors, our individual ability to cope comes back to how comfortable we are with change in our everyday lives. We largely underestimate our resilience and our ability to bounce back. At first we assume the worst, as shock and fear overwhelm our senses, but once our minds have had time to process the information, we showcase our strength and agility by moving towards solutions and actively responding, even in the most extreme situations. Our conscious minds are processing machines, and once the adrenalin has worn off they're wired to assume control and inform our post-crisis decisions.

When I look back to the weeks we first sat in front of our screens mesmerised by the unfolding chaos of Covid-19, I remember the fear I felt for my business. I became laser-focused, blocking out all peripheral noise to focus on finding solutions that would ensure the business survived. I knew I had to get out of the weeds and step up to bring confidence back to my team. I compartmentalised my fears of failure and buried them deep so that I could focus on developing ways forward and ensuring our survival.

## Taking charge

Covid-19 was not the first time I had experienced this super-fixation and a single-focus mindset. When my son was first diagnosed with cancer, my initial instinct was to hand over all other life and work responsibilities so I could focus entirely on his recovery. I desperately wanted to pass over the reins of my business to someone else. There were many times when I wished my business away, as it felt like the only way I could cope. But I knew in my heart that I had to find a way forward that would enable me to protect my business and my staff while I looked after my son.

These feelings of failure and immense turmoil peaked during the many times I couldn't attend his appointments, or when other members of my family stepped in to be at his bedside when my schedule wouldn't allow it. The conflict between being a parent and a boss can cause significant anxiety, forcing you to question whether you are doing the right thing. It starts from the moment you have a child, when the balance of work and parenting creates a push–pull tension with no one solution. Thankfully longer periods of parental leave and greater workplace flexibility are alleviating some of these pressures today. When my children were young, I had to learn to be comfortable with the decisions I made, knowing that I was not less of a mum because I chose to work.

Life is full of compromises and times we're forced to prioritise one action over another. Anyone responsible for young children, ageing parents, community initiatives or significant personal projects must learn to develop workarounds to squeeze all aspects of their life into each month. Fitting together the pieces of the puzzle comes with many trade-offs, and you must constantly prioritise day-to-day decisions. When chaos reigns it can feel as though the pressure of life will never ease, but these phases are usually limited to a finite period, and in time the juggling act comes to an end.

I cope with stress best when my mind is busy. Others need space, and some need to be surrounded by people. When my son started his cancer treatment, I coped by doing what I love: keeping busy. I became a committed researcher on his type of cancer, Hodgkin lymphoma, and I would spend every available minute researching it and its effect on teens. Initially, this was a way for me to better understand what he was going through, but it soon became an interest in treatment options. Before long I was developing insights from different medical studies to determine the pros and cons of different treatment plans.

I never set out with the intention of questioning my son's treatment, but in my readings I came across a French medical study on a treatment plan that was seeing great success in teenagers. My son was part of a different study and medical protocol, meaning his treatment was part of a specific study that was being run across the world by a number of hospitals. As I became well versed in his cancer treatment, I began to understand how many options were being deployed around the world. Once I had enough data and evidence, I presented my findings to my son's oncologist. Thankfully he didn't laugh me out of his office and he was interested in my findings. He agreed the new treatment protocol I had found looked promising, and he committed to having the data peer-reviewed and consulting with other researchers and specialists. My son's medical team accepted the evidence of this newer study as a valid alternative to the current approach, and my son's treatment was changed. Had I not become a competent researcher as part of my master's study, I would never have had the confidence to search and then present medical data to a medical specialist. The benefits of becoming an adult learner had paid off in ways I could never have predicted.

I am eternally grateful that my son's oncologist was open and willing to listen to other ideas, even from a complete novice. By the end of 2015 my son got the news we had all been waiting for: he was cancer-free and in remission. He was a cancer survivor. The day-one scan when he'd first been diagnosed had showed his internal organs lit up like a Christmas tree. His final scan had lost the bright-light neon effect and looked like any other healthy fifteen-year-old's body. That day, when he was given the all-clear, my heart did somersaults. The relief was instant. As we walked out of the hospital together we hugged tightly without saying a word. We felt like heroes, and we knew we were the lucky ones. We were acutely aware that many others who had regularly shared that teenage waiting room with us had not been so lucky.

## Preparing for the challenges to come

Life has taught me that nothing is forever. The best times and the worst times all come to an end. It is the times in between that shape who we are and what our legacy will be.

Adversity is a catalyst for innovation and progress, but it also builds strength. For many people, Covid-19 has been the most challenging event so far this century. It won't be the last. Millions of people around the globe have lost loved ones to the virus, others have been torn apart by closed borders or health risks. Hundreds of thousands of businesses have closed their doors on what were once lucrative enterprises, forcing people to find new work.

From a distance, Planet Earth is a serene, marble-like planet moving through the solar system. In a plane we see rivers and mountains, roads and city lights. On the ground we are individuals and small collectives, each of us facing our own personal turmoil and adversity. Perspective is everything. Context is important.

Many of the challenges we will face over the coming years and decades will be universal to all people on our planet. In response, we must become increasingly adaptive to navigate climate change, population growth, and the health and education needs of the global community.

Covid-19 has taught us how adaptable we can be. It has shown us the importance of learning new ways to solve emerging challenges. It has amplified our need for meaningful connection and shown us that we can prioritise new threats even if it means taking on significant personal financial risk.

In the coming years, certain predictions will play out. Industry will continue to automate many job processes. New skills will be needed to actively participate in the job market. People will work well beyond the retirement age of 65. Education will be reinvented to be more responsive, more personalised and more relevant to future workforce needs. New technologies will shape societal shifts and attitudes. We will all adapt the way we live to mitigate the effects of climate change. Life will become a series of adjustments to respond to new situations.

It is easy to fear this impending uncertainty and fragility, but I know we are far more adaptable than we give ourselves credit for. Back in the early years of The Mind Lab, surrounded by young children experimenting with technology that they had never seen, I saw how capable we are of finding solutions. Children don't set limitations on their capabilities unless someone tells them something is beyond their reach. Your worst enemy is the voice inside your mind who tells you what you can and cannot do. I wish that our childhood curiosity could stay with us forever. As adults we impose limitations on ourselves that define so much of what we experience. I believe the world delivers what you have the capacity to deal with, even when at times it feels unjust and inequitable. Some people are born to move the dial and to lead progress, and some people are passengers. Until we really test what we are truly capable of, we don't know how many great things we could achieve.

We are all, for the most part, creatures of habit. We like our routines and falling back on pre-existing skills – doing the same job, going to the same restaurant, listening to the same music. But if you were to take the moments in your life when you tried something new, look at what you learned and calculate your return on investment, you would find that experimentation and stepping out of your comfort zone comes with significant benefits.

In 12 short years of compulsory schooling, there are tangible gains for every hour spent processing new information – literacy, numeracy, reading comprehension, the ability to recall important formulas, events or theories. This all comes down to less than 480 weeks in the classroom. Once our compulsory schooling is done, we must open our minds to new ideas and concepts that will give us the best returns and help us thrive in life.

For the most part, knowledge is intangible. We can't see it or measure how well informed a person is just by looking at them. We can't evaluate how current their skills are, or count how many biases or out-of-date assumptions they're drawing upon to inform their decisions. We certainly can't evaluate how they will cope under pressure or how they might adjust to unforeseen change and disruption.

Committing to prepare for the road ahead is an investment in your own future happiness and resilience. Let your curiosity lead for a while. You may just find there is nothing stopping you from achieving all that you dream.

## CHAPTER 11

# The future of work

It's a matter of learning

## Outdated, outmoded, outpaced

No debate topic elicits a more emotional response than the future of work. So much of a person's life can be traced to the decisions they make between the ages of 15 and 22, when they decide who they're going to be. The school system aligns a student's choice of subjects with their career options, then they are filtered at tertiary institutes according to their specialisation. The career-mapping process starts well before we have formed any real view on what we love to do, how we like to work or where industries are heading. Before most young people have worked a full day in a job, we ask them to narrow down their subject choices from a smorgasbord of options to focus on just a few key subjects that will determine their university eligibility, which programmes they can enter and even whether they can demonstrate their intelligence by passing exams.

Forgive me for being disparaging, but this system is deeply flawed.

Our education system, the very thing that is designed to teach, inspire and develop our future leaders, scientists, technologists, doctors, innovators, politicians and community champions, is failing under pressure. The biggest challenge we all face in the future of work is that there are very few aspects of the education system that have transformed in response to the way we work, learn and live in the twenty-first century. While Covid-19 has been the single biggest circuit breaker in the past 200 years of learning, the majority of schools and institutes are fixated on getting back to normal. Students today are informed by multiple different sources of information, and many are deeply immersed in online communities, social networks and topic-based online groups.

Speak to an average 15-year-old today, and you'll find they typically have a good grasp on international politics, climate initiatives, and societal shifts including those that relate to race, gender and age. They often have a side hustle involving an online exchange of value, such as developing virtual assets for gaming, trading cryptocurrencies or selling products in an online marketplace. They are the always-on, learn-as-you-go YouTube generation. If they don't know how, they google it. They have significant communities and social tribes online built around common interests and understandings.

But in the classroom or lecture hall, the education system continues to assume that teachers are highly skilled communicators and the only source of knowledge in the room. Continuing to teach students using a one-to-many model, with a single teacher in front of a class, is not only flawed, it's deeply arrogant. It's like saying the chief executive is the only source of good ideas in an organisation.

Given how much we now know about how people learn and apply new knowledge, it's unfathomable that we still expect students to take notes so that they can recall facts for exams, which are then used to evaluate their comprehension and understanding. I don't know about you, but the recollection of facts has provided me with very little benefit in my career, especially as many of the things I've learned over the decades have since been superseded by better intelligence and new understandings.

There is no justifiable reason to continue scheduling education around traditional working models. People across the world have discovered 'just in time' learning, turning to their smartphones for clarity or answers. Unstructured learning is being delivered everywhere. It's live from expert practitioners on highly advanced education platforms. It's on podcasts, in videos, and on social media and a multitude of streaming services. Outside of classrooms, learning is increasingly personalised according to style or progress, and it's supported by artificial intelligence and detailed datasets of student behaviour. We can plan for our careers in the future by learning at industry-specific meetups, through online micro-credentials and nanodegrees, all without once stepping into a classroom.

But even in the bright light of day, where big changes in the workplace are starkly evident, traditional education models remain strong. Is it that schools and institutes of learning are blind to the future of work? Or is too challenging to adopt new modes of delivery within traditional structures and mindsets? Is it too hard to contextualise content in today's fast-moving world?

Sometimes it feels like we're allowing outdated models of learning to continue because we want our children and younger staff members to go through the same process we did, because it's familiar and it served us well.

Perhaps employers are part of the problem. If we continue to focus on very specific education pathways and qualifications to source new recruits, I fear the education system will continue to align to our needs. We will never see the benefits of diversity of thought and the benefits of inclusion unless we abandon the assumption that the best people to work in our organisations and teams must fit a very specific mould.

The current education system is not moving closer to the needs of the future workforce. In fact, it could be said that we are facing unprecedented future failure. The 2020 New Zealand Initiative report *NZ Education Delusion* stated that in 2019 just 58 per cent of New Zealand students attended school at least 90 per cent of the time. Today's students are choosing not to go to class in increasing numbers. This is not only a trend in senior classes – it starts while students are still counting their birthday candles in single digits. Whichever way you cut education data, the issue is clear: if we can't make education accessible, meaningful and relevant for our students, our children's future potential will suffer.

I acknowledge that changing an entire system is incredibly hard. Shifting mindsets is difficult too. We all show resistance and even hostility when our tried and tested ways are pushed and challenged. I am often asked what my biggest dream would be, and it's the easiest question in the world to answer. I want decision makers to look to the future and map out future needs – skills, sectors, jobs and capabilities. Then I want them to reverse-engineer how we get there – how our children get there, how all children get there, how reskilling adults get there.

## Commit to keeping up

The future of work is not a job for life, a nine-to-five day or a daily commute to the office. I would go so far as to predict that, before we roll into the next decade, we will all work fewer hours but with significantly higher levels of productivity. Our workplaces will be a mixture of locations, determined by the type of work we are doing. We will use advanced immersive technologies to be in virtual rooms with our colleagues and our customers, and we will all be actively learning as part of our commitment to stay informed and relevant. Industries will have morphed in response to carbon restrictions and an increased commitment to sustainability. The workforce will be less defined by age and experience, and more by capability. Teams will be geographically distributed, and will include staff and contractors who live offshore. All major business processes will be automated, and strategic decisions will be made using real-time data and advanced algorithms that run theoretical scenarios to validate decision-making.

We are tasked with preparing for the future in ways we never expected. We should be focused on when our current skills will become redundant and when we'll need to build new skills and understanding to support our career progression. All adults should become highly attuned to the signals of change – the indicators of where sectors are heading, and what disruptors are doing differently.

We all need to become comfortable being out of the decision-making seat, and being an onlooker to new conversations. The sidelines are the best spot to learn. Whether you're leading a team, setting out on your career or starting a new job in a different company, being able to understand new information will be the most critical component of personal and professional development.

But most people don't see themselves as students. Many are quite happy to trade on what they've learned through experience or on-the-job training. The problem with this is that there is so little scope to move beyond the familiar. We seldom focus on the practice of negotiation as an area of learning, but no one can sit at a negotiating table without understanding the views of the other party. We can't overcome differences of opinion to create long-lasting, impactful change without each party truly knowing what those differences are. The willingness of all people at the table to comprehend the views of others is crucial to finding agreement – it's the first step.

Committing to developing a process of negotiation takes time and energy, but the benefits speak for themselves. When two parties compromise in a way that makes both feel heard, there won't be one true winner – and that's a good thing. Whether you're listening to the views of a supportive community, or a challenging colleague, or even working through the dissolution of a marriage, the desire to win can be one of the most important characteristics to quieten. Life is too short to win at all costs. If you want to move long-held views forward and be part of meaningful conversations about the future, it's important that no one walks away feeling the process was biased, predetermined or unfair. If you find yourself at the table and you have some influence, getting all parties to agree to see the process through goes a long way towards finding a resolution.

## If we play by old rules, we'll get old solutions

Trying to move the dial and support progress in education has been the biggest challenge of my life. We should be open to progress, inspired by better insights and an understanding of what works, but I face many stakeholders who are hell bent on defending the status quo. Some of my biggest battles have been fought with policymakers or indoctrinated leaders who depend on the world staying the same. I have lost sleep, shed tears and been worn down by the lack of progress in these systems of conformity, and I am not alone. Frustration is growing across all sectors at the inflexibility and protectionism of some legacy organisations. To move mountains, and to make sure that our future reflects the changing views of society and industry, we all need to take responsibility for calling out the powerful systems and people who stand behind closed doors. By having hard conversations we can drive new outcomes that will improve the world.

I struggle to understand why we're supporting a 200-year-old system that is well past its use-by date. There is no obvious gatekeeper or dominating authority, no one source of control – fixed thinking exists across the entire ecosystem. Yet we continue to support a model that's no longer fit for purpose. I have to assume that, over time, views will change and systems will come to better reflect the world outside the education system. I hope that emerging voices and instruments of change have the strength and ability to promote the benefits of a more responsive system. Read any news headline: the industrial world is over. Kaput.

Our jobs are morphing, and our problems are too. If we play by old rules we will get old solutions. We need to tackle the systems that we know are irrelevant to support the next generation and the one after that.

I have always been a fighter. I feel deeply for people who are failed by systems that have not evolved. I'm prepared to step up and challenge myself, and I'm committed to asking harder questions and requesting better answers. One step forward and two steps back. I know that in time I will simply run out of the fight, but I'm hopeful that I'll outpace the detractors. I know a generational change will lead new conversations and a more significant collective of voices will step in.

My challenges are tied to the worlds of education and technology, but leaders around me have their own battles to fight. Even the most change-resistant person would be hard-pressed to ignore the upsurge of technological transformation occurring across the globe. We're experiencing extreme and unprecedented demand for skilled people. Covid-19 might've been the catalyst to drive mass-digitalisation of businesses, or it might be a by-product of the 2.8 billion members of Gen Z building better, faster ways to live – ultimately the cause is irrelevant. Every major technological evolution has had a tipping point driven by societal shifts, and technological advances do not dissipate over time. We have a global talent-shortage problem. For every year that passes, the available talent needs to grow. An 18-year-old today simply doesn't understand landline phones, printed newspapers, scheduled television, libraries, taxis, bank branches, nine-to-five office hours or even email. Profound changes have occurred in these sectors, as tech giants have replaced the original sector leaders. Apple was never a telco, Netflix was not a TV network, Spotify didn't own a radio station. If technology hasn't already disrupted your sector, it will. And it will not be a known competitor who causes this disruption; it will be a technology-based organisation that has reimagined what you do to be more efficient.

We are seeing advances in connectivity, and significant improvements in video-based calls, e-commerce retail, online banking and access to essential services, that would not have been possible just a few years ago. QR codes and Bluetooth tracking are yet another technological advancement that has changed the way we think about data.

We all need be mature in our thinking and know when and how to break old ways, so that we can move forward using new practices. How many parts of your life are you wearing like a much-loved blanket that's hard to let go of? How many views do you have that you're doggedly holding on to for no reason other than that they're familiar?

We're all on a journey of transformation. Every day we learn and see things that influence how we imagine our future. We will all fight internal battles as we let go of some of the structures or practices that are part of who we are. But we'll all evolve and progress one way or another, either because we actively participate or because we're dragged across the line. Being proactive about who you want to be doesn't mean choosing the right subjects at school; it's about who you fight for, who you back and the battles you choose.

Your future is what you shape it to be. All I can hope is that you form your view with an abundance of knowledge, and without limitations that are comfortable and familiar.

## CHAPTER 12

# Confronting mortality

## Take nothing for granted

## How old will you be when you die?

I recently completed a survey from a company capturing anonymous information about retirement savings. The first thing asked was, 'How old do you expect to be when you die?' Good question. I'm not sure there is a more confronting or difficult question to answer. Should I look back at the age of my grandparents when they passed away and add a decade or two? Should I factor in my health, diet, stress levels and work?

I have thought it through a number of times, and my view is that, all things being equal, I should easily see my hundredth birthday. I assume I will live to be this age as I'm an optimist. My grandparents lived into their nineties, so I figure that, with all the benefits of science, genetics and technology, I am here for the long haul.

Most people think otherwise. Despite scientific data showing a significant increase in longevity and projections of a rise in the number of people living beyond 100, the majority of people assume their time will be up much earlier. When I'd completed the survey, I got to see the results. They were surprising. The majority of survey participants selected 75–80 years as their expected age range for death. Even today this is a very modest number for people who do not have underlying health conditions.

It's hard to imagine living for 100 years. It means acknowledging that a person's retirement period will be around 35 years. How do you plan to financially support 35 years of living between 65 and 100? Does that mean 35 years living off savings? Most people have less than ten years' worth of retirement savings.

I was so fascinated by the findings of the survey that I took screen grabs. I wanted to read the responses of my peers. Most participants said they had no investments and few savings to support themselves in retirement.

I did the maths.

Let's say Person A retires at 65 years of age and dies at 80. Nearly 20 per cent of this person's entire life will be lived in the period after they retire. If Person A owns their own home and has modest living costs of $50,000 per year, they'll need to save a minimum of $750,000 to maintain their modest lifestyle. To me, this is concerning not because it's a big number (though it is), but because Person A needs a job between now and when they're 65. What do they imagine that job will be if they don't embrace new knowledge and skills?

Imagine you're employed as a retail manager. You're currently 45 years old. There are 20 years until you retire, but already you can see that e-commerce, data personalisation and online marketing are changing the way people buy products. Now it's 2027 and you're 50. Everything is automated and your industry demands skills in data analytics, inventory management, digital marketing, crypto and digital payments, international logistics, and procurement and customer relationship management. You focused on business as usual and you haven't learned new skills. There are now 15 years until you retire, but your role has been made redundant. You apply for new roles but they too require you to have experience and commercial understanding of digital processes and automated procedures. Your earnings between 50 and 65 are now compromised. Your income and savings reduce over the final ten years of your career, meaning you arrive at retirement with significantly lower savings than you'd hoped.

This is not a far-fetched or unlikely scenario. It will be the reality for many in Generation X and many millennials as we move further into the twenty-first century. Over the coming years, the need to adapt and integrate new digital tools is a certainty. We're now in a period of history known as the Fourth Industrial Revolution. The only constant is the increasing rate of change. The jobs and roles in your future will be nothing like the ones you imagine.

Officially, I have 15 years until I retire. I know I will continue to work much longer than this. Maybe I'll hang up my current hat and head into a creative field. Or maybe I'll become a leading expert on quantum mechanics. Strangely, I can't think of a reason why not. Who says technologists have to be young?

We know the average person is living longer – much longer. I grew up hearing the phrase 'three score and ten' as the life expectancy of the oldest people in my family. Had I lived 100 years ago, my time on earth would pretty much be up already. My children, based on the projected averages of current data, will all live to be around a hundred years old. That's a lot of uncharted terrain to cover in one lifetime.

Death is not a subject that sits easily in any conversation. It's uncomfortable to imagine your own death, as any acknowledgement of your eventual departure comes with the reality that there is only a set number of days ahead to achieve all the things you want to do. If you spent any time on Instagram in 2021, you may have seen an advert for a life calendar that's based on a person's likely life expectancy. The calendar works like a Dutch auction, counting backwards from the high point of days left, to the single-digit numbers when all you have ahead is borrowed time. I've thought about the effect this calendar must have on people. Is it designed to be a carrot or a stick? Would crossing off the days on a reverse calendar be a motivating prompt or a morbid reminder? My view is, to truly live, we have to acknowledge that at some stage in the future we won't be here. Our world will be passed on to the next generation, and then the one after that. What world will we leave to our grandchildren and great-grandchildren? This is a subject of heightened importance and responsibility in an era of climate change, as we are asked to make decisions that will have an impact well beyond our time.

As we all hope and plan for the future, our optimism and enjoyment will be challenged in the years ahead by the loss of loved ones. As older family and friends age, I find myself in a slow grieving process. Emotions shift as each birthday rolls round, marking that the years of life ahead are reducing. But I hope that the years to come will be the years that define me most – beyond the hustle of raising children, work and constant decision-making. After retirement, we have more space to enjoy relationships, learn new skills, see new places and spend as much time as possible with our loved ones. First, though, I have a whole lot of living and learning to do, as to fully embrace my future I need to make great decisions right here, right now. They will have a greater influence on my future and my children's future than any commitment I make in 30 years' time.

I'm also aware that there are no guarantees in life. The lives of some of my friends were cut short. They never had the chance to make the decisions I have, and I mourn that they didn't get the chance to see all the wonders the world can bring.

## Life is precious

The sudden tragic loss of people close to you can never be truly imagined. In an emotional sense, we bank decades of living for everyone we love – the idea anyone's life may be cut short is unthinkable. But how does death fit in a book focused on thriving in the future? There is some solace to be gained by sharing parallel experiences, sure, but no two feelings or emotions are alike.

The reality is that death is part of living. It is part of feeling and part of knowing. Sometimes the people we love have their lives taken away early. They are friends, family and loved ones who will never have the chance to think about retirement, drive around the country in a campervan staying with their children, or receive their gold card for discounted tickets.

We should remember that there are people among us who prey on our vulnerabilities or use force to gain power over us. And even if we escape death, tragic violence can still befall us at someone else's hand. Too many of my friends have found themselves at the mercy of others.

In 2000, before New Zealand had a games industry of any scale, I met a friend working in technology. Tech was not her first career – it was a massive pivot from her role as a professional ballet dancer. Prior to our meeting, she was firmly focused on her future as a dancer, and she was very talented. As part of her dance training, she became a very competent martial artist and frequently entered tournaments where she took on men two or three times her size. Her presence as a highly ranked woman was not always appreciated at these events, especially as she was also a dancer. At one tournament, before the referee had even stepped on the mat, her opponent jumped her and smashed her leg in multiple places. She was never able to dance or compete again.

We assume everyone around us will play by the same rules,

but evidence to the contrary is everywhere. Not all stories have happy endings.

We seldom talk about death in business, but it has a profound effect on our staff and their world when loved ones die. At a governance level, boards talk about 'key-person risk' when they plan for the possibility the person in charge might suddenly find themselves unable to lead. Truth is, 'key-person risk' is a polite way to talk about the risk of a leader dying unexpectedly.

In my team of around a hundred people, seven staff members had parents die while I was writing this book. Tragically, one beloved staff member died unexpectedly too. Each time our entire organisation went into a period of mourning as we all confronted the reality of loss, the reality of our own mortality and were reminded how precious life is. We assume our family and our friends are invincible, and that they will be with us forever. The alternative is too hard to process, so when tragedy strikes our lives are forever changed.

A number of my personal friends have been killed at the hands of others. It's a statistical anomaly that cannot be explained. Sometimes it's as though life has been paraded in front of me, then callously and traumatically taken away with little regard for the impact it would have.

My primary school was tiny. It had six classrooms and a small field to run around in. We had a small library, a school office and a shed for sporting equipment. The bus that took me to school was red and the driver was always happy. I didn't know the driver's name, or at least I don't recall it now, but she often whistled as she drove the bus from my rural farm to the primary school on the outskirts of town. I grew up with the same small group of friends from the time I was five years old. We were an oddball collection of 1970s children, and every year we met up in a different school classroom as we progressed from room one through to room six. The headmaster was already old when I joined his class as a ten-year-old. He had bright eyes and a smiling face, but he also had Tommy Tickler, a thick leather strap that he kept in his top drawer to ensure we all tried hard to do the right thing.

Primary school was a time of discovery. I learned I could paint, write and play a musical instrument. I loved sports and the library. I even loved my drawstring homework bag, which contained new books to read and maths or spelling to practise. I was a quiet and diligent student, and I enjoyed being part of something tight-knit and predictable.

My teachers were the only unpredictable part of my schooling. They had vastly different personalities. Some were kind and showed infinite patience, and others were jaded and consistently disinterested. One of my teachers had taught my father as well. She was so small that even as a child I stood taller than her. She always carried a long wooden ruler that she would bang on our heads if we stumbled over words on the reading mat. We had another teacher whose surname I found unpronounceable, and I was scared of her from the day she arrived. Once, I caught my knee on a sharp nail sticking out of my wooden desk. Blood gushed out and soon started flowing to the floor. I covered the wound with a handkerchief until it was soaked through. Eventually the murmuring of the other students caught the teacher's attention and she came to my rescue. Up until that moment, though, there was nothing in the world that would've given me the confidence to disturb her 'quiet time'. My fear of her reaction was real.

I had crushes on some of the boys; I loved their sense of adventure and the physicality of their life. My friends were my world. We would gather at my home and play with our dolls, making tea parties for Barbie and Cindy. Life was simple, small and stress-free.

One of my closest friends lived near the town swimming pool.

The pool was the hang-out joint for young people throughout the summer months. I learned to swim there, in the full-length Olympic-sized pool. My friend lived a few doors away, and I would often meet her at her home before we raced through the turnstile at the pool's entrance and straight into the cool water. She had an older sister and they were both so much cooler than me. My friend was the first to get wedge-heeled blue sparkly sneakers. I couldn't believe there was anything so beautiful.

A number of years later, her murder became front-page news. The murderer was another classmate from my small primary-school class. All three of us stand in the same class photo. 1979. Her death was horrific. She didn't have a chance. It was premeditated, vicious and final. When she was murdered, I hadn't spoken with her for years but it didn't lessen the sadness. She was part of an innocent time growing up in a world that saw little change. Her life ended before her own kids got to experience the same innocence she had once lived with.

I left my small town at 14 without ever saying a proper goodbye. I consciously decided against a farewell, as I wasn't sure I was really going for good. I was moving north to the big city with my mother, and I didn't know whether it was a permanent decision as I wasn't sure if I would fit in. It turned out life in the city suited me. I liked the increased pace of living, having new ways to spend my free time and making new friends.

When I was 17 and living in London, a very dear high-school friend regularly sent me letters by airmail, sharing stories of her life back home, talking about familiar places and friends we both knew. Her letters were one of my most rewarding gifts in those early days of living in a new country. She was on a mission to become a great designer. I was in awe of her talent and hoped in time she would join me in London. But then suddenly the letters stopped. I asked about her in letters I sent to mutual friends, but my questions went unanswered. During my very infrequent phone calls home, I asked my family if they could reach out to her to see if she was OK. But there was no news.

London was a million miles away from the life I had left behind, and I took in every opportunity that a big global city offered a curious 17-year-old. It wasn't until my first trip home a couple of years later that my family told me my friend had died in a hit and run, just a few hundred metres from the school where we'd attended art classes together. The driver was never found. My friends and family had collectively decided not to tell me, worried that I would find the trauma of losing a friend too difficult without a support network around me. I understand their rationale – this was a time before mobile phones, the internet or social media. Life was lived in discrete, disconnected pockets; it was vastly different from the uber-connected world we know now.

While living in London I reconnected with a school friend who had returned to the UK after a stint living in New Zealand. She was studying at a college in Bath. I moved into her dorm room and slept on the floor on a thin foam mattress. The first night I arrived we went to a party with a tropical-island theme. It was below zero outside, but inside we wore sarongs, hula skirts and coconut-shell bras, and we danced to the Gipsy Kings. The Mexican–Hawaiian mash-up was lost on us; we were just happy to be living life to its fullest.

During my time in the UK, my friend's mum became my rock when I was homesick. I would travel by train to her small but perfect home a couple of hours outside London. Here, I reconnected with my friend's older sister. We had also been at school together, but she was two years older. We'd sit up late at night talking and reminiscing about our school days. I was so thankful for her friendship, and I loved hearing her stories.

A few years later when I was back in New Zealand, the older sister reached out. She was returning to New Zealand to see friends and travel the country. I was so excited and couldn't wait to reconnect. We never did. The night before she was due to fly out, her jealous boyfriend stabbed her to death.

Another friend met a similar fate while living in Europe just a few years later.

I struggle to understand how the people we trust, and in many cases the people we love, can sometimes be the same people who cut short our future. I fervently wish that women in volatile relationships were better supported to get out. The extreme power plays and dominance of some people should never get to be a deciding factor in how long someone lives.

The most recent loss of a friend is so current that the brochure of photos and programme for her funeral is still next to my bed. I can't throw the programme away as her smiling face beams out at me. She is a beautiful woman I will never forget.

Her funeral was one of the hardest experiences of my life. She had an open coffin, but I couldn't view her. I knew the body in the casket was so broken that, even surrounded by hundreds of roses to mask her injuries, she was unrecognisable. Her attacker was well known to her. She was stabbed and beaten beyond recognition. He is now in the justice system; she lives as a feeling of love in my broken heart.

Life delivers so much joy and hope and possibility but, in return, it sometimes brings the most extreme sadness. I know that every day is a new day when good things can be achieved. I know that most people are extraordinarily good. We can't live in fear; we need to live with optimism and hope for what we can do in the time we walk this planet.

The commitment to doing good things shapes me. I take nothing for granted, and I know that being a woman leading organisations committed to helping others to learn and develop is the way I drown out the derailers. When you reach into life with open arms and an open heart, you will see and hear things that don't come with guidebooks. Ask anyone working in organisations created to improve the lives of oppressed and disadvantaged people, and they'll tell you stories that will break your heart and change your perspective. Life is not a box of chocolates, and, for many, each day that passes is a process of survival. We should never assume we understand the burdens of others or that we know what it's like to walk in their shoes. But we also shouldn't fear stepping into hard spaces. We are capable of remarkable things, and we can dig extraordinarily deep when we need to. A step to help others may just save a life.

Many things in life stop us in our tracks. Thankfully there is a societal shift occurring right now, and people are standing up in greater numbers against those who oppress people and hold them down. I am encouraged that many strongholds of the past are crumbling. A new generation of leaders is creating a different future, one that doesn't have room for old hierarchies of power. Young leaders are confident in their fluidity and authenticity, even if that means showing their vulnerability. I love that I can say 'I don't know' or 'This may not work' and people respond with support and a commitment to try. Mediocrity, or a life without passion for what we do, is life's least rewarding pathway. Fighting for a cause, supporting an initiative and committing to making a difference provides us with the perspective, insight and understanding we all need to make good decisions. Living without direction does not.

At my primary school, children who stepped out of line, or students who didn't learn at the same rate as everyone else, were threatened and punished. The industrial world believed in a very narrow view of conformity and uniformity, and it was supported by a small group of influential people. This environment disadvantaged many. Now that we have discovered the benefits of original thinking, innovation and experimentation, we should celebrate diversity and our differences. People with very different experiences can come together to solve problems.

We have moved a long way in a short time. Young people increasingly view transparency and openness as key attributes of good leadership, spurred on by the millennials rewriting the leadership rule book. If we can continue to celebrate people who are open, and who share their feelings and emotions, we may have a chance to break the cycle of violence and domination. Positive change will only come when we focus on destabilising cultures of power and control.

I know not everyone is on the same page as me. Some people think the younger generations are too soft, lacking in resilience and too focused on equity and the environment. I'd rather be surrounded by compassionate, thoughtful people who want to make a difference than alpha personalities who command an audience and respect.

All of my friends who have died in unspeakable atrocities have been women. I wish this wasn't the case. I wish murder, power and greed weren't part of any life. But we can't live with our blinkers on. The power plays of the past still exist and they prevent many people from living the lives they dream of.

I recently attended a full-day self-defence workshop with 24 other women. It was a Sunday, and we were in the basement car park of a nondescript commercial building opposite the main city hospital. The women ranged in age from around twenty to mid-fifties. Our instructors didn't mince words. They were there to help us learn how to defend ourselves against an assailant, and they meant it. We pushed each other up against concrete walls using throat holds. We were attacked from behind and pushed from the front. We lay on our backs on the floor and we punched hard into punching pads as we tried to get away. We twisted out of neck holds and slammed our arms against our partner's. We knew the bruises would come, but we also knew that learning this way was necessary if we really wanted to be able to have a chance of defending ourselves should we ever have to.

By the end of the day I was physically and emotionally exhausted. In the days following, I thought about the absurdity of even needing self-defence classes. There have been significant changes over the decades, and we now solve problems and build our futures with a far greater commitment to all members of our communities, but have we really evolved? Do we still value the wrong things? Do we focus too much on benefiting a few instead of positively impacting many? At a macro level, data tells us we are becoming smarter, healthier and wealthier, but the trade-off is profound. Inequality is more significant than ever. Will big business respond differently in the future, in light of what we've discovered about ourselves while fighting Covid-19? Will younger generations win better outcomes and access for all? Have we evolved enough that my children won't see their friends die at the hands of others?

How old will you be when you die? How are you planning to live your life in the future? You might be planning for life with children, or for when your children move out of home. You could be leaving university and thinking about the type of work culture that best suits your values. Maybe you have finished your full-time career and you're focusing on the activities and pursuits you will have in retirement.

There's a number for every year of your life on a bingo card. Almost. The number 90 is the highest bingo number. It doesn't feel like that's where my story will end. I'm hoping that at 90 I'll be surrounded by great-grandchildren, watching them use the technologies of their time to connect, learn and socialise.

We talk about death and the later chapters of our personal stories so seldom. I hope that this changes, and that we all take time to imagine the possibility of the future in all its beauty.

## CHAPTER 13

# Your online brand

## Do we really know what is real?

### What happened to privacy?

The influence and effects of social media and our ever-connected world are not limited to young people. You might think that there's nothing in your online activity that's a threat to your privacy, but this is likely not the case. Today, as our careers progress, our views, images and thoughts become increasingly public. More often than not, your online profile will be defined by others, and if it's negative or features misreporting, there's little you can do to correct it and present the truth. Until a couple of decades ago, privacy was only a passing consideration in business and in our personal lives. There was an unwritten expectation that the people we worked with and those who surrounded us wouldn't share information that was confided in trust. Physical privacy in our homes was of low priority, and could be achieved by simply closing the curtains. Now, with a few clicks, we can discover who a person is, what they stand for, what causes they support, how they spend their time and even where they live. It's easy to discover radical, highly conservative or unorthodox views, and these will be judged.

Recruitment companies regularly dig deep into your online activity – they find your comments on product reviews, your social media posts and any affiliations you have. Whether you are applying for a new job or considering a role in governance, the discovery process extends to how you spend your life outside of work.

Most people don't really know what their online profile says about them. Too often they assume that what is said online simply disappears over time as more and more content is published. On a broad level this is true. People who want to bury past behaviour often contract social media experts to populate online media with new content, so that old or regrettable comments are lost in the noise of information. But if someone is very specifically looking into your life, they'll be able to recover information going back years.

When you think about your own online activity, how would you define it? Are you a recognised thought leader who posts regularly? Or is your online profile limited to a few random posts from a couple of years ago? Are your personal profile pages on social media private and only visible to trusted friends and family, or is everything you do open for all to see and view?

You online profile is likely to be the first view of you that a potential employer, new colleague or a date receives. If you're a millennial, much of this knowledge will be well understood, but adults who grew up well before their first Facebook post understand their digital footprints much less clearly.

It goes without saying that your future you is a product of your past you. While our real-world actions are limited to a single moment in time, the online world is permanent. It's an inerasable record of all that we do. Even if you have no intention of sharing photos from your night out on the town, or the protest you went along to on Sunday afternoon, others in attendance are unlikely to give it a second thought as they tag you in their posts.

Many future and current employers are likely to undertake a full review of how you live, both in and outside of work, and they will evaluate how your online profile could be interpreted by others. The nuances of your language, tone, attitude and opinions are all fair game when it comes to business. Even the most meaningless sharing of a post, or comment on a friend's photo, could be forming a picture of you that is totally removed from reality.

If you choose to live out of the limelight, away from social media and off the grid, you are still being watched. You are observed by satellites, tracked by your phone, your location is geotagged. You are listened to by your devices and influenced by your online searches, and your information is sold to advertisers when you purchase something. The information you hear, read and see is biased at best, fake at worst, and opinions and radical conspiracies are often represented as mainstream views. Finding the truth takes time, and validating information is complex. Yet somehow most of us can detect which information is the most reliable and most likely to be credible. We have become attuned to paying attention to the details that we once accepted at face value.

Without thinking about it, we accept that our spam filters will separate important emails from junk ones. We appreciate the viewing algorithms that make valid suggestions for the next Netflix series we should watch based on the shows we've previously viewed. We rely on sensors that are part of the internet of things to regulate the temperature of the spaces we work, or guide us as we move through cities. Using technology and anonymised private data to improve our lives is now par for the course.

There are so many things we once paid close attention to that we no longer think consciously about. My children have never used physical maps to navigate while driving their cars. They have never seen a fax machine or a pager. They have never had to fast-forward through a music cassette to find a song they like. They have never answered a landline phone in our house or taken a photo and waited a week to see it.

They have also never experienced real privacy. They are watched in every moment of their lives. They are tracked by each e-commerce search then targeted by an algorithm if they abandon the purchase once the item is in their shopping cart. Their personal data is sold and on-sold multiple times each day as codes describe what they might be interested in buying, experiencing or supporting.

How often do you think about who you share your private data with? How many times have you filled out an online form for a mortgage broker, health service or insurance company that includes your date of birth, financial data, home address or health information? Even riskier, how many times have you sent this information to a third party by email?

We are all guilty of sharing our information on websites and in emails without truly understanding who is accessing it and how it's stored. For example, the comprehensive data you emailed to your mortgage broker now exists on your email system, your phone, their phone and their email client. The passwords that you and they put in place are the first and possibly only defence against your information being accessed by a third party. It's unlikely that someone will intercept or access your data for illegal purposes, but we have to assume they could – in the same way we lock our windows and doors when we leave our homes.

Privacy has become subjective and contestable. It is becoming more and more difficult to protect or control what happens with your data. Cybercrimes are on the increase and the pain that breaches bring can be long-lasting, emotionally devastating and in many cases life-changing.

Even when there is no malicious intent, people are often thrust into the spotlight for reasons that seemed harmless at the time:

unfortunate dance moves caught on camera, a leader who shows their true colours after mistakenly expecting everyone would observe the 'no phones allowed' rule. We now live in a time and place where transparency extends in both directions. On the one hand, we are rewarded for being open and willing to share our lives outside the office, but, on the other, we risk being vilified if our views are misaligned with what people expect. The person you are at home is the same person the world expects you to be in public, and vice versa. Sharing our identities has come with a cost. Our private lives play out much more publicly than in any previous generation. Judgement is fierce and failure becomes open tender for public scrutiny.

Sharing our lives has become an industry, an obsession. Influencers, many of whom are famous for being infamous, are channelled into our media streams flaunting the new, must-wear jeans or the most awe-inspiring mascara. Our children are being marketed to from the moment they can turn on an iPad. Be this, don't be this, like this, but not this. Be hotter, smarter, richer or more popular. Recent reports from Instagram and Facebook ex-employees throw light on the practices the company uses to drive clicks to the most sensational stories, further contributing to the increasing rates of mental health issues, including the rise of anxiety and diminishing self-esteem, among young people. Doomscrolling is a full-time occupation. Most teenagers spend over eight hours a day online – it's not surprising that the constant bombardment of content is shaping their views and sense of self-worth. The people who create content purely to grab attention and data often prey on our insecurities, including the desire to belong, to feel valued and to understand.

When I was growing up, my views were informed, moderated and developed by those around me. I read newspapers in which journalists and reporters spent significant time and energy validating claims before making statements or accusations. This is no longer the world we live in. Privacy is now subjective, and the physical world and the virtual world have collided. Reputation and trust earned over a lifetime of hard work can be squashed in a single post or a misplaced judgement.

## Your business is everybody's business

Businesses are now held responsible for their decisions, including their choice of brand imagery and product claims. Backlash and negative publicity are likely to come from massive online audiences rather than known customers. But hype and sensationalism catch eyeballs: the more controversial or misaligned a business's views or decisions are in comparison to the mainstream, the more likely that business will suddenly find itself headline news. Truth never gets in the way of a good story.

Talk to any senior marketing executive about their career and how their decision-making processes have changed over the years. In the past, marketers judged how a new advertising campaign might land in the market by testing it across a representative group of target audiences. The majority view was the determining factor. If most people liked the idea, the campaign would be greenlit and the promotion would go ahead. Today the views of the entire marketplace are significant as we now recognise that messaging is received very differently by different people. Marketers must understand how and why messages, decisions and suggestions are interpreted by different audiences. If a campaign or message is perceived as biased, ignorant or irrelevant, the market will respond, and in many cases they will respond very publicly.

Transparency, authenticity and being able to stand by your decisions have never been more important. Work decisions are no longer ring-fenced by office hours or even by physical office spaces. Every decision you make is connected to you as an individual, and your online presence crosses over from work to home. If you make decisions that are ill-informed or unfounded, the online response has the potential to make your life crash and burn overnight. A lifetime of good work can be undone by one late-night tweet.

Let me use an example. You own a well-performing four-year-old business selling skin products. The business is expanding internationally and its online profile is growing thanks to Instagram, Facebook and Pinterest. In an effort to highlight the benefits of the product, the marketing team choose to emphasise certain ingredients as having medicinal advantages. These claims are added to the advertising and a new campaign is launched. There is no obvious risk – the campaign doesn't include customer before and after shots, there are no product guarantees, and you don't use clickbait headlines with promises of restored youth overnight.

Initially the market responds well. Sales are up. Then, one lone online comment questions the authenticity of the medicinal advantages. They link to a controversial article about the lack of evidence to show this ingredient has medicinal advantages, and even more concerning the environmental impact that harvesting this natural ingredient is having on the local ecosystem.

The post sparks a reaction. One person after another joins the conversation. More and more people jump in, but now they are questioning your choice of influencer and her public persona. They ask you for evidence to prove the product has medicinal benefits and ask whether there is any background to your claim.

For a few hours the online dialogue continues flaring up and you find yourself stepping in to defend your business. Now your private world is part of your public world. Your personal social accounts are soon being publicly trolled, and you change the settings on all your accounts to private. The heat on your business lasts only 24 hours, but the damage is done. You feel attacked and beaten down. The entire issue ran its course over a single day, but the impact is drawn out. You and your team feel exhausted, exposed and downhearted. Even when the dust settles, the emotional impact of the online opposition continues sparking up. Your staff read social media posts from the comfort of their homes, in places designed to be separate from the stresses of the workplace. They find themselves heading down rabbit holes as they follow the comment threads to posts about your business on other sites. Their downtime is infiltrated, and yours is too. Your privacy feels compromised both in the office and at home.

Now, this might sound like an extreme example but it's not. We have all seen what happens when the owner of a business or an employee makes a truly outrageous or ignorant claim on social media. We have seen businesses close after an out-of-touch boss goes on a rant, and we have seen mass customer retaliation in response to employees sharing conspiracy theories or outrageous claims.

Privacy in your business cannot be assumed. My advice is to stand by every comment you make. If you would be uncomfortable being called by a journalist on a Sunday afternoon to answer questions about something you wrote, then it is probably best left unsaid.

Part of me grieves for the past, when our actions weren't scrutinised by everybody. I am thankful that there wasn't a camera capturing every stupid decision and misspent moment of my youth. That is a luxury my own children will never have. An entire generation of young people now curate their images and critique each other's lives, photos and experiences. I have a few fading magenta-coloured Kodak moments in old photo albums that I am pleased will never be seen by a mass audience: my 1980s perm, questionable fashion choices and unflattering reminders of social gatherings.

Today, Google ultimately decides which version of myself the world will judge me on. Clicks determine which of my activities, images and projects people will first see and then use to understand my character. There is nothing I can do to influence or contribute to this perception. We are the sum of many algorithms and the target of well-crafted clickbait.

Even seasoned company directors receive training on social media and how to prevent being targeted by disgruntled customers or unhappy shareholders. This training generally extends to keeping yourself safe in the office, at home, at airports and in public, as a negative reaction to a board-level decision can lead to physical or online intimidation. Have we become more intolerant and uncompromising towards people with views that differ from our own? Or have social media and the internet removed controls on information that were taken for granted in the past?

## Getting your facts straight

One issue with the rise of social media is the proliferation of new forms of content, including blogs, tweets, memes and videos that inundate the internet and dilute the value of factual information. Most people have high levels of trust in search-engine results – it's a big ask to expect individuals to evaluate whether an algorithm might be manipulating their search results. Over time, tools designed to identify fake information will be more widely deployed, but until then we have few ways of detecting inauthentic actors and false narratives before we too spread fake news.

Competition for our attention online is intense, and we often take the path of least resistance. We all need to understand that information and knowledge are increasingly influenced by algorithms that prioritise search information based on our prior online behaviour. We are all subject to the influence of predictive analytics and code specifically designed to determine the information we will find most agreeable. Our views are validated by common, repeating themes, regardless of whether they are true.

In my world of postgraduate education, teaching now goes beyond holding discussions on complex societal shifts and the emergence of new information; every new student cohort starts out with explicit guidance about where they should seek and source their information. In contrast to previous times when research was sourced through books and journals in the university library, today's students wade through literally millions of search results, seeking authenticated information from unknown sources.

Most professionals have a good understanding of the manipulation of data through fake news or sensational headlines that serve no purpose beyond capturing eyeballs and clicks. Promoted stories that pop up in our web feeds or on our social media prey on our desire to be part of a breaking story – the more scandalous the better. These stories aren't lightweight and harmless, though; they're highly manipulative. Some lure us in using eye candy, or the chance to improve our bodies, minds and lives. Some use lurid come-ons to seduce people with controversial topics or conspiracy theories. Others use the faces of well-respected leaders and link to stories with no connection to the image. Clickbait doesn't advance knowledge – it does nothing to help our minds traverse new ideas and concepts. Instead, it feeds the reptilian part of the brain, triggering basic instincts using 'you should see them now' images of celebrities.

Surfing the internet for stories that make you feel better at cost to someone else is addictive. Most of the content on the internet is unfiltered, unproven, unjustified and untrue; less than 1 per cent of all online content has been indexed by Google. The majority serves no purpose at all other than capturing your attention and details so that your searching behaviour can be sold on to advertisers.

The deep web holds most of the content we produce, from forms to emails, intranets to academic papers. But even if this content was indexed and searchable by Google, it would bring little value to a mainstream audience as it is of little relevance to most people. (The deep web is very different from the dark web. The dark web often features in news stories on cyber breaches, ransomware and online crime. It is known as the home of choice for highly illegal sales or traders of dubious products or services. The dark web can't be stumbled upon or searched for. It's a playground for deviants and people who don't wish to be discovered.)

Just because something looks authentic, don't assume it's based on fact. Even legitimate publications use complex online marketing techniques to attract readers. There is an algorithm that knows just what it will take to get you to click the right key. Conspiracy theorists are known to infiltrate legitimate research forums and sites using academic papers and journals that target audiences through the promotion of fake studies. At my organisations we work hard to ensure students cross-check sources and become highly attuned to papers that appear to lack the academic rigour common to peer-reviewed journals.

## Baring all

On a lighter note, or at least it's much funnier now than it was at the time, I too have been the victim of a privacy breach. Around 2004 I had a general health check and my doctor suggested that I go and have my skin checked for melanoma. If you didn't grow up lying in the sun for hours smothered in baby oil, the idea of proactively checking for melanoma might seem a bit over the top. However, like most of my contemporaries, it's become standard practice for me in penance for my misinformed and misguided youth.

Back in 2004 a melanoma check played out like this. You stripped down and stood very awkwardly in front of a skin technician, who scanned your body for spots or marks that were slightly odd in appearance. Each unusual-looking spot was captured by a very high-tech digital camera so that the image file could be reviewed by a specialist skin doctor. Unfortunately this process took time. As I stood trying to be as comfortable as possible in the bright lights of a medical office, I told myself that the embarrassment I was feeling would soon be over and that I was only subjecting myself to such an intrusive process for my health.

After I left the clinic I thought nothing more of it, at least not for another week. Around seven days later I received an email from my internal tech team. The subject line read: 'POTENTIAL MALWARE ATTACHMENT: Skin-mapping results.' This was a time when email inboxes weren't under constant threat of phishing attacks and viruses, so our organisation had the IT team manually check flagged emails addressed to individuals on staff to ensure the email-scanning software didn't block legitimate attachments.

As soon as I saw the subject line my heart stopped. I could see there was still an attachment on the email and I knew it had been cleared by my IT team. I reluctantly opened the email to see a message from the IT team that said, 'Cleared email with attachments. Note we did not review the contents.' Which of course meant they had.

Twenty-two low-res photos of close-ups of my body were cleared for approval by a team of young male technicians. I wanted the world to swallow me up and to just simply disappear. The idea that photos of my body designed for medical evaluation had been 'cleared' by my tech team led me to have broken sleep for weeks afterwards.

Needless to say, I didn't respond to their email and I never raised it with them either. For a few months we'd pass each other in the corridor with a polite nod, our eyes fixed on the floor. I never went back to that skin clinic again.

I understand the practice of sending images has since been replaced by a secure backend system, where patients can log in to view their photos. I now use an AI skin app called SkinVision that does the same thing but, instead of relying on the opinion of one specialist, it uses the results of millions of scans to identify which skin spots are potentially high risk. It's the very best in technology, it costs less than $100 per year, and I can scan as many spots as I want. Better still, the real people who review my file see just a small area of skin at a time. No booty shots needed.

## Rules of engagement

Any privacy and information-security skills I learned earlier in my life have little relevance in today's digital world, which needs much higher levels of sophistication. I grew up thinking of privacy as a right. In my office, my home or my car, I could simply turn off the rest of the world and know with certainty that I was in control of my private life. Today we leave digital footprints wherever we go. When we walk into physical spaces, Bluetooth and Wi-Fi are tracking our every move. Every day we trade convenience for the sharing of our data. We have come to expect online services be provided at no cost, but these companies recoup their investment by capturing your data, making it harder for you to stay private. Some might see this as a win–win, but others see it as an intrusion on our human rights, the erosion of the right to live a life free of external influence.

What you share online today will influence how people form their opinion of you tomorrow. As with the decisions you make in the real world, you must be deliberate about what you do and mindful of possible interpretations and their consequences. Even the language you use is up for interpretation – shorthand, quickfire responses are often misunderstood, when nuance gets lost in translation.

We should view the rules of engagement across all aspects of our lives in their totality. Be consistent in your messaging and online reputation over time – it will always be the best defence against a misinterpreted post or poorly thought-out response.

Your online profile can be as active or limited as you choose. Curate it well, and online media could become one of your greatest channels of connection. But step forward carefully – what starts as a side interest can easily become all consuming. It is important to be vigilant about who you engage in conversation with, as in the virtual world deviant behaviour and manipulation are not so easily recognisable. We regularly invite people into our digital worlds with little or no knowledge of who they are and what they stand for. The media is filled with stories of people whose lives have been unravelled by serious cyber harassment, identity theft and the misuse of data, images and information to extort money or power.

Step online with your eyes wide open. As much as possible, protect your data, your privacy and your movements from the view of virtual connections. Treat people you meet online the same way you'd treat someone you met at an in-person conference: it's great to chat and connect, but you wouldn't necessarily share your family photos and details of where you live.

The majority of the world is now connected through mobile phones and the internet. We spend more time connecting with others online than we do in person. Who we are in the real world has become a subset of who we are, as is who we are connected with online. Most business people have at least ten times more connections online than people they actually know offline.

Stay focused on the relationships and connections that make you feel your best. While it may take a little more time to plan a catch-up with a friend in person, the endorphins and joy that come from real connection will always be far superior to scrolling through clickbait.

# CHAPTER 14

# Sister wives

## Find your cheer team

*'The typical expression of opening Friendship would be something like, "What? You too? I thought I was the only one."'*

– C. S. Lewis

Friendship has a huge part to play in life and in business. Everyone should have a group of people they trust to guide them through difficult times and challenging decisions. I wouldn't be where I am today if not for my remarkable friends and colleagues who've stood by me when self-doubt or self-defeat set in. Many of my decisions have been made in coordination with the advice from a row of supporters on the sidelines. I've made other decisions assisted by a passing comment or feedback from someone I've admired. Many of these people won't be aware of how much they've helped me, but those in my close-knit team know just how valuable their influence and support is. Great friends and family members are more than advocates and supporters; they're the people who know you the best. They are your safety net when the world delivers lemons.

I have a group chat called 'Sister wives'. The name is apt: these five extraordinary humans are like sisters to me. I can lean on them no matter what. We didn't go to school together, we don't share common university connections, and our children didn't grow up together. We are a curated collective that just happened to gel. I'm not sure exactly how the universe lined us all up and put us together, but I am forever thankful it did.

Most friendships are built on chance encounters, or through regular interaction at work, playing sport or at social events. My friendship with the sister wives fulfils none of these criteria. And we didn't know how much we needed each other until we met.

We first connected on a weekend getaway that one member of the group coordinated in 2015. We barely knew each other outside our tenuous links in business. I must admit I tried to talk myself out of going. Strangely, while I'm comfortable travelling alone to off-the-beaten-track locations, the introvert in me doesn't naturally gravitate towards socialising with unfamiliar people. But I have learned to catch myself when I'm declining opportunities and stage a personal intervention. I redirect my mind mid-thought and recognise I need to stay open. So, seven years ago I accepted this somewhat unusual invitation to meet a bunch of women for a weekend getaway. I had no idea just how much of a life-defining moment it would be.

You could try to set up a weekend get-together with people who hardly know each other a hundred times, and the likelihood is it wouldn't work out. But somehow, on this particular weekend, we all arrived with the understanding that connecting with a group of people open enough to say yes to the invitation was an opportunity. We sat and talked about our lives, our work, our families and our challenges. We had so little prior knowledge of one another that we had to start from the beginning, and we filled in the gaps as we went. As the weekend unfolded, we began to understand each other's motivations, values and goals. We talked about things that even our oldest friends didn't know. We got to tell our stories from beginning to end. We are six very different women, with six different journeys, but we share a common set of values and the ambition to make a difference.

Every one of us has a big job – heading listed companies, government agencies and private enterprises, and championing community initiatives. There are 12 years and an impressive amount of living between us: international jobs, multiple marriages and divorces, significant health scares, major wins and huge losses, children and now even our first grandchild. We are all somewhat nomadic, due to our international work commitments and a common love of travel. Sometimes we're passing ships, bumping into one another at an airport or at an event where there's little time to talk. But knowing these friends are there is the best support I could ever ask for. Nothing is off-limits in this group. There's no judgement, no expectation of how or when we'll engage and no assumptions about what each other needs. We accept each interaction as a unique event. If I was to write a message in our group chat saying that I needed help, they would be there. There's no jealousy of each other's successes or judgement of our failures.

## Breaking out of the everyday

We all carry biases, and we defer to autopilot more often than we're consciously aware we do. This behaviour is most pronounced when we respond to new information or hear opinions that don't reinforce our personal views. When I'm teaching, or even speaking from a stage, it's easy to see how people in the audience react when new information lands in their minds. I can literally see in their expressions whether they're open or closed to new concepts, and I can see them evaluating their willingness to learn a new idea.

There's no logic in these human responses – they're not age-based, gender-based or skewed to a particular type of person.

We get to choose whether we show up and accept new information every day. Some people are open to change and new concepts. Others are not. Learned behaviours are reinforced over time, often through group agreement or institutionalised groupthink. When our minds respond automatically, we can miss the opportunity to develop and grow, and to experience activities that will benefit and enrich our lives. We must learn to identify when our immediate response to a situation is self-limiting and habitual, and re-evaluate if necessary to willingly accept the chance to try something new.

Being able to stop yourself from coming up with reasons not to try something new is an extremely useful skill in an environment that is constantly changing. In today's world we are continually confronted by new information, scientific advances, new behaviours and opportunities to do things differently. Accepting this new information doesn't happen automatically. You need to consciously make a call as to whether you are willing to include this new information in your mental filing cabinet of things you understand.

Think back over recent technological advances – space travel, gene editing, quantum computing and new forms of payment including non-fungible tokens. New neural pathways have formed in our brains to make sense of all these new things we are seeing, hearing and learning about. If you want to break habits, it's important to surround yourself with people who bring new perspectives and ideas. Without the disruption of changing personal interactions, varied schedules and unique experiences, it's all too easy for one day to merge into the next.

We all feel most comfortable surrounded by people like ourselves. It's one of the easiest forms of positive affirmation we have. It's also appealing to avoid disagreement – agreement requires less energy, less thought and less time. However, by wanting to be surrounded by people who are highly agreeable to us, we miss out on the very conversations that would enable us to grow.

There has been significant research undertaken in the workplace that proves the financial, cultural and social benefits of a diverse workforce. Having a team of people with different experiences, skills and cultural backgrounds, and people of different genders and ages, is key to high performance. We grow and extend our capabilities through direct exposure to different ways of thinking, working and problem-solving; we can't get there if the same repetitive mental processes or similar neural pathways are continually reinforced.

But the benefits of diversity are not limited to the workplace. Being open to change and being confident with new ideas are skills ideally introduced at a young age, through friendships in primary school and sports. If we are to learn how to evaluate new concepts, it's critical that we surround ourselves, in all areas of our lives, with people who bring unexpected perspectives or unfamiliar experiences.

Friend groups like the sister wives help us build personal strength and an understanding of others. Trusted friends can question your logic and ask you to explain your decision without fear of conflict. Some people do this better than others – some groups of friends have loads of debate without consequence, whereas others would never disagree with the dominant view in the room for fear of reprisal. Even within families and cultures tolerance for divergent views or debate differs. Some families are so aligned in their thoughts and behaviours that they avoid the friction needed to debate important issues. When all conversations stay in the range of agreeable safe topics – sport, kids, entertainment and social events – repetition of conversations becomes the norm.

I have also learned that tolerance of disagreement can be very localised, down to a team level. Within organisations, team leaders will set unwritten rules that determine how vocal an individual can be before they are managed back in line. Some teams and organisations have hierarchies built on the ability to control decision-making, ensuring that very few new ideas and very little feedback makes their way to the top table. In these environments, change is extraordinarily slow. Inputs from the broader workforce don't receive the oxygen they need to develop. This means that great ideas are missed and opportunities for growth diminish. Staff turnover in these organisations is more likely to come from discontent with the culture than a desire to change roles.

The proven value of diversity doesn't mean that having people around you who are a lot like you is a bad thing. Familiarity also has its benefits. We often gain mental strength by sharing openly with loved ones who don't need an explanation. Family and close friendship bonds are often built on similarity and the comfort of routines, rituals and behaviours. There is significant benefit in having a group or groups of people who know you so well that you don't need to say a word in their presence.

My sister wives are like this. We know each other so well that we can all be in the same room but happy in the silence of common understanding. We can be intensely active in our communications or go days without more than a cursory hello. What makes this group so powerful is the high level of trust we have with one another, which has never been breached.

## Bravery is not a solo pursuit

The happiness and strength that comes from real connection is hard to define. We all desire and need people we can lean on, but we don't often give much thought to who would surround us in our ideal group of friends.

A year after the first weekend getaway of the sister wives, I was asked to speak at the International Monetary Fund in Washington,

DC, at a women's leadership conference. They asked that I speak on a topic that would be of relevance to an international gathering of female leaders. I opened my talk by putting up a slide on the big screen that featured the faces of my sister wives. I talked about the importance of kindred spirits and active supporters to personal and business growth. I talked about the difference between the support of spouses, childhood friends or family members, and the power of a group of very specific people who support you as part of a strong collective. I spoke of the advantages of developing a close-knit group of friends who could be constructive with their feedback and a sounding board when you needed clarity in your decision-making.

At the end of the conference, we came together for a social gathering. As I met and chatted with the other attendees, I realised how many of them, all highly successful women, had experienced the isolation of leadership. They confided in me that they felt separated from their staff, as they were expected to know all the answers and to show constant strength. They had difficulty communicating work challenges with their social friends, especially with those who didn't have the same level of responsibility at work. Many of these women said that too often they were making important decisions without ever discussing the topic outside their formal work meetings. They were developing strategies for the future of their businesses with only the sole input of themselves.

It isn't easy to form friendships when you're constantly busy with work, travel and family. We expect that when we move to a new city or start a new role we'll make new connections. But as we spend more time online and working from home, we need to be more deliberate about building friendships, which may include becoming comfortable with letting others know when we're looking for new connections.

My sister wives help me with decisions that need airing with multiple audiences. Their views don't always align, and they will sometimes give me feedback that is counter to what I'd hoped for. No one person has all the answers, and no one situation is like another. Our partners, husbands, wives and families are heavily invested in us and our happiness, but they are also biased. Sometimes they will unwittingly put limitations on our potential by trying to protect us from risk or stress. Leadership and personal growth needs the support of many. It takes a village to raise a child, and it takes a team of supporters to develop a leader. There is no weakness in seeking the views of others when making decisions.

Hardly a day goes by that we are not asked to make a decision that will influence or affect others. The more senior you become, the more people will look towards you for guidance, and the more significant this responsibility will feel. Many people feel anxious about having to make a decision that feels right, but is in opposition to what others want. These are the hardest decisions to make – they can feel like no-win situations. Anyone who has had to make staff members redundant, or who has recognised that a high-performing member of the team is actually detrimental to the culture of the organisation, will know how tough these decisions are. Sometimes the Band-Aid needs to be pulled off quickly and other times it's important to take it slow and build a case around a big decision. All decisions are better for being aired with others; often we find clarity or have our views swayed by talking something through out loud. Having a group of allies you trust is paramount.

The active curation of groups of women has been a common feature of my life and career. My first group of kindred spirits formed in 1998, not long after the birth of my first son. I was general manager of Media Design School and I recognised that I needed a group of people who I could bounce ideas off. I reached out to four of the smartest women I knew. We were all still in the early stages of our careers, but we had big plans for the future. One worked in a leadership role in a museum, one had a senior role in corporate public relations, another was an account director at an advertising agency, and the fourth had just left a corporate gig to head up visitor experience at the local America's Cup Village. They became powerful influences in my life as I embarked on the exciting but challenging path of a first-time business owner. Back then, we had very little communication between our scheduled gatherings but we knew that we had an instant sounding board if we ever needed advice.

We are all still connected thanks to the power of the internet and social networks, but since those early days when we first met we have scattered across the country and the globe to new communities and careers. We all became mums, and we all became leaders within our respective industries. Our journeys followed many different squiggly routes. Today, one of these friends is a group head of brand in Reading in the UK, another is the VP of marketing in a big firm in San Francisco, one works in philanthropic fundraising in a small town in New Zealand, and the friend I see the most regularly recently made the decision to leave the corporate world and live on a rural lifestyle block. They have all been incredibly influential in my life, and they saw my ability to become an entrepreneur when no one else I knew was. I hope they know how important their friendship is to me.

Between this group and the formation of the sister wives, there was one potential group that fizzled out before it ever really got established. I was the chief executive of Media Design School and my life had become overly shaped by my work commitments. I was always online, on planes or at airports. I missed the company of close female friends who understood what it was like to juggle a busy work life with multiple other commitments. I decided to bring together a group of women who I admired. This group was truly eclectic – the video game designer, the interior designer, the sales director and the up-and-coming local politician. One of the members of this group is now the prime minister of New Zealand. Today Jacinda Ardern is one of the most recognised leaders in the world. Even 12 years ago, when we first connected, it was obvious Jacinda was on a trajectory to do something incredible. While she was relatively unknown at the time, a steady stream of fangirls and boys acknowledged her as they passed by our dinner table.

This group of women never met up again as a collective, but I stayed connected with each of them individually. It turns out that, even with the best intentions and the desire to stay connected, it's really hard to align the diaries of five women on separate missions. Today we all run significant organisations. I'm not sure that any of us at the time would have believed for one second that we'd end up where we are today. I haven't run the numbers, but the probability of five random women meeting for dinner in 2010 and later all becoming CEOs seems against the odds. More unlikely still is that one of this group would become the boss of an entire nation. Life is like that. You never know where the journey will take you, or who might encourage you to be your bravest self.

Together with eight extraordinary women leaders, I am also a partner in a company called On Being Bold that has the explicit purpose of helping other women leaders excel. Once a year we host a conference for hundreds of women who are inspired, challenged and guided by other women leaders. I love this day. It's a highlight in my annual calendar. We hold the conference just before Christmas, when we're all feeling excited about the year finishing and looking forward to the chance to spend time on holiday with our loved ones.

The timing of the event is not accidental. Every year has a start, a middle and an end. As a general rule, most days in the calendar lack specific significance, but the big themes that mark the changing of the seasons or holidays connect us to symbolic events. The end of the calendar year is a chance to tidy things away, to reflect on progress and to set new targets.

The Bold Steps conference brings together 800 women in a single room. The first thing you notice on entering is that it's noisy. Really noisy. Something about the excited chatter of women connecting with friends and colleagues for a special day of celebration seems to amplify the volume by magnitudes not seen at other events. The second thing that separates this event from other conferences is the openness and transparency shared from the stage. International idols, local heroes, the governor general, the prime minister, female CEOs from New Zealand's largest listed companies, and the chairs of world-leading organisations take to the stage and open their little black book of business successes and failures. There are no sponsors, there's no hard sell. It's just a curated group of leaders who understand the power of sharing.

I am part of the team behind this event, and we first came together in 2016 – I was not a ring leader but a ring-in. This group is high stakes in the world of intimidation: two dames, a CEO from one of New Zealand's largest listed companies, and multiple board chairs and board directors from the who's who in business. This group has the most influential people in our country on speed dial. Even though I sit on boards and have received my fair share of recognition, including being appointed a Companion of the New Zealand Order of Merit for my contribution to education and technology, I still feel like an imposter in the presence of these women. I find myself feeling like a kid watching a private conversation between a group of idols. I've tried to convince myself that deciding not to work in the corporate sector doesn't mean I'm less important, but I've been unable to truly do so. The idea of success is still very much tied to big business. There are thousands of online and print publications dedicated to profiling the glamour of large enterprises. My world in tech and education feels scrappy by comparison, and a constant hustle. Because my work is technology based, my vocabulary is different from the corporate offices where I often work as an advisor. I am an outsider who views the world of business through technological advancement and adaptation. My lens looks nothing like theirs.

Whenever we get together, I'm inspired by this group of women for very different reasons. They are all strong, smart and powerful, and they're trailblazing pioneers in their fields. I didn't have to work my way up the corporate ladder, or be subjected to most of the barriers they faced as women working in male-dominated sectors. As an entrepreneur I have formed my own teams and built my own organisations from the ground up. I have never faced discrimination for being a female boss. I have never been made redundant. I don't oversee multiple millions of dollars each week on behalf of shareholders. Our responsibilities are very different, but they all come with the need to make good decisions.

The other very special day in the annual calendar of this group is a leadership event for female students in their last year of high school called Dreaming Big. We host this event at my work, and we invite female students from every high school in the region. It's not an event designed for the head girl or the academic superstars from each school; it's for the quiet leaders who have demonstrated high potential but prefer to lead from behind the scenes. I can relate to these young girls – I was one of them. I wasn't a leader at my high schools, I didn't wear achievement badges, I wasn't in the school production or a leading sports person. I quietly chipped away at my studies and led from the back. I was a good student with good grades, but I had no desire to put myself anywhere I'd stand out.

When I see this group young women come together, I wonder whether their generation will be the one to break down the final strongholds of traditional success. Will their parents still encourage them to be bankers and lawyers over climate scientists and social workers? Will our children's children aspire to create different types of value and to move away from the old constraints of roles where value is derived by annual returns? I have two young nieces who are just starting their primary-school journeys. They are polar opposites in character and in their approaches to life, but they are both part of a new generation shaped by possibility. There is nothing in their future that they see as out of scope or off limits. There are no gendered careers or limits to their aspirations – they simply have never seen or experienced anything that would make them think that there are still ceilings to break through.

What I know now more than ever is that we all need the love and support of great friends to do brave things. No one person is able to summon the strength that a team of friends or the strength of family can provide. Regardless of what we do, we all need extra-large doses of encouragement at certain times in our lives. We're all surrounded by people undertaking difficult tasks, from those working in the community on grassroots initiatives to those in research labs working to find cures to diseases. We should never underestimate an individual's ability to change the world, or at least the lives of others. I know first-hand how beneficial it is to receive a reminder that what you are doing is important and valued – it can be a simple text of encouragement or an email acknowledging that you're making a difference. I am forever grateful for all of the support I've received over my career. I never take this for granted. We sow what we reap and vice versa. When was the last time you picked up the phone or sent a note to someone who is doing something you admire? Even a short word of thanks has the ability to help people move mountains. There have been many times when I've been on the last hurdle of a major project and a simple note of thanks has been enough to push me to the finish line.

Winston Churchill once said that courage is the first of all virtues because it is the only one that guarantees all the others.

We all have the ability to plot a bold course, forge new ground or be decisive in a time of uncertainty. As the world adapts to new challenges, courage has become an indispensable attribute for effective leadership. The leaders steering their organisations and communities forward while seizing new opportunities for impact and growth are some of the most influential people of our time. Adapting quickly and stepping forward with certainty, even if internally you're terrified of failure, can reduce anxiety and fear in others.

When you're looking to lead with a sense of possibility, friendships and networks of supporters are a great source of encouragement. Many models of leadership fail to mention that you will sometimes have to explicitly state that a vision comes without a compass. With every destination, there are multiple paths and many may lead to dead ends. If you lead by saying that there is only one possible path to success, it can create the impression that the road to success is certain, or that the direction chosen will be the path of least resistance. If you build a community of supporters that you keep informed with your plans, you will have a network of people who support you when things go off the rails. Success and comfort seldom come together, but having a network that understands and supports your cause will provide the safety net you need when tough days get tougher. All great causes and successful initiatives are headed by people who have a strong sense of leadership.

The first step to making bold change is to focus on the purpose and reason for your goal, and why you're hoping to make changes. Before you lean in to the task at hand, take your team or supporters on your journey and make them aware of your biggest concerns. In my organisation, all staff meetings follow the same principle: I explain the opportunity so that everyone can see the big picture, and I talk through the timeframe and the risks, then I share my fears and aspirations.

I have grown comfortable sharing my thoughts while they're still developing. When I have other people's input, I'm able to see things from different angles and from different perspectives. I look back at my earlier career and I recognise I saw things in absolutes. It wasn't until I learned the art of compromise and negotiation that I found the rewards and benefits of bringing many trusted people into the development process. I find myself welcoming the challenge of those who ask hard questions. I have a village of people I know I can rely on to stand by me, as they know why I do what I do and why it matters to me.

Self-confidence is an important attribute in great leaders, but not if it comes with the overconfidence that assumes you're better alone. Curiosity and the desire to do things better will attract greater support than having a fixed opinion or an inflated sense of your decision-making abilities. In many of the companies I work in as a futures advisor, I see a disconnect between the executive and other staff. In every instance I believe in transparency over secrecy. If you open up your own world and share your vulnerabilities, you will be able to proactively seek opinions and the people around you will feel they can safely offer advice or put forward a suggestion.

Friends, supporters, backers and colleagues are essential to the success or failure of a project, business or movement. No man or woman can operate alone if they are to do great things. Having encouragement and a cheer team who will come to your defence is critical to your growth and development. If you're looking for help on the road to success, never underestimate the power of the human spirit and a village of supporters.

Before I met my sister wives I didn't know that I needed a group of friends who would help me be brave. I now know bravery is not a solo pursuit; it requires the general support of many and the unfaltering encouragement of a few. We need courage to follow our dreams and aspirations, particularly if we're walking away from what we know to seek something better. Doing brave things alone is much more difficult than doing them with the emotional encouragement of others. In our families, and particularly as parents, support can be the difference between happiness or sadness, success or failure. Uncompromising, limitless love is one of the most important human needs. I'm lucky to have my family and my friends to lift me when things are tough, and in turn I provide support when they need it. In the absence of a family of personal champions, there's an abundance of people to meet and connect with. It's just a matter of stepping outside of your comfort zone and being open to connection.

## CHAPTER 15

# Partner woes

## Back yourself

### Let there be thorns

It's 2017 and I'm standing in a small boardroom presenting a financial retrospective, looking back on a year of great progress in my business. We have experienced significant growth and the impact we're having is being noticed. Local and global awards have generated an impressive collection of trophies for the reception wall. Highly skilled and passionate staff are having a hugely positive impact on operations, and our systems and processes are functioning better than ever before.

Where I am standing is not my boardroom. It is the boardroom of the 50 per cent shareholder who invested in my business at a time when we were rapidly expanding. I haven't met the majority of these board members before – they are a different group from when I presented the annual results last year. They are an eclectic mix of independent directors and they look worried. As I set up my laptop and plug into the screen, I can sense their tension.

I don't know the source of their troubles, but it's clearly present. Their brows are furrowed. The energy in the room is dark and heavy.

Back in 2014, I accepted an offer of investment in my business from a government-owned entity. At the time it had felt like an exciting opportunity to activate my plans to expand, moving from educating school-aged children to developing postgraduate studies. I had been in the education rodeo long enough to know that there were many benefits to having a large, established education player sitting at the table with me. Running a start-up as a sole shareholder carries a lot of personal risk: burning through cash flow, burnout and missed opportunities due to a lack of bandwidth. I looked forward to building the credibility of my senior team by accessing senior board members with experience in education.

Before I'd entered the boardroom today, I had been looking forward to sharing our organisation's updates after a highly successful fourth year of trade. We have so much to celebrate. So much for my team and I to be proud of. But my optimism is short-lived. As I stand at the front of the room, backlit by the large projection screen, an invisible sledgehammer swings down from above, slamming through the numbers on the screen.

My excitement at sharing good news is shattered. This group is in for the kill. They ask me to skip the pages of curated images, the successes, to move to the section focused on financial returns. I stand my ground, trying to explain the importance of the impact we are having on the education sector, but the group closes in and demands I go straight to the spreadsheets. As I project the profit and loss for the year, my focus becomes razor sharp. A barrage of questions is hurled at me. They go on the attack and demand bigger, faster, more profitable returns. I stand disbelieving as my good-news story about their successful investment is met by a tirade of financial demands: diversification, growth, increased profit and reduced costs. It's a text-book interrogation by a group of shareholders looking for better returns. But this isn't a group of investors looking for better dividends. This is an independent group representing the interests of a government-owned institute that by legal standing is a not-for-profit entity. I have no comprehension of the underlying catalyst for their unreasonable demands.

I look directly at them and try to talk about our many educational successes and how our institute is changing lives and preparing people for the future of work. But my words fall on deaf ears. The aggression within this group is overwhelming. I watch as a culture of chaos and blame plays out in front of me. I look around the room for a friendly face, focusing on the only two people I know in attendance. They look back at me with blank expressions. Whatever they know, they aren't about to share. I conclude my presentation and sit down.

I look around the table at the collection of board members. It's the first time I've had the chance to really look at them. There is real trouble in their eyes. I can't understand where their distress is coming from.

After leaving the meeting I call one of the executives who was present. 'What's going on?' I ask.

'Don't worry,' he says. 'The new board members are just trying to grandstand and show their presence in the meeting.'

I know better. Something is up and even as I'm speaking to him I know that whatever it is, it's somehow about to impact my world.

It doesn't take long for me to get my answer. The following week I wake to the sound of an early-morning text from a colleague. My business partner is in a $50 million-dollar hole and they are about to experience a full intervention. The board will be disbanded and a commissioner put in place. Suddenly the benefits of my government-funded financial partner look like one of the greatest challenges I will ever face. I know that they will be required to sell their shareholding in my institute as part of their debt recovery.

I am faced with a new and unknown business partner buying out their shareholding – or I have to find a way to buy them out.

## Dig deep and hold out

With the benefit of time and more information, I have since gained far greater clarity of what went on behind the scenes leading up to that day in the boardroom. Prior to the interrogation, our business partnership had been strong. Our two entities were aligned in our education philosophies. We had slightly different priorities, but we worked constructively to move forward in unison. I welcomed the addition of representatives from their executive team to my board, and we recognised each other's strengths and capabilities.

But in the months prior to their financial failure they became distracted, and their previous openness and willingness to engage began to diminish. In hindsight, there were clear indicators that things were not going well, but at the time they didn't share a single word of their troubles with me or my board. The failure of their business, which led to their need to urgently sell all their shares in my organisation, didn't register until the day I read it in the news headlines. We had joined forces four years before, and by this stage we were teaching thousands of postgraduate students in multiple locations around the country, and we were growing.

They had bought shares in my business at a very early stage, when our valuation was low, and they sold when the value was high. My buy-back of their shareholding hurt. They profited even in their demise.

Amazingly, over the weeks that followed, as I sold my family home and negotiated with the bank for support, I didn't receive a single communication from anyone at my partner institute beyond the formal requests from their lawyers or appointed business valuation agency. They didn't acknowledge once just how much they had thrown me under the bus. One day we were all playing happy shareholding families, and the next I was steadying the boat by taking on debt and trying to convince my team that everything was going to be all right.

I wish I could say that having a large and seemingly impressive investor always leads to good things, but it often doesn't. In my work I am often approached by young founders seeking advice in relation to investor behaviour, including hostile takeovers, overly dominant influence or exclusion tactics at the decision-making table. For any entrepreneur running low on operating cash flow, an injection of financial support from an investor or partner will often appear to be the only way forward. However, the very nature of early stage, pre-revenue start-ups is that they're yet to see their real long-term potential. Diluting the ownership of a business in the very early stages, when it has significant upward momentum, can become a founder's most regretted decision. A positive business trajectory in the early stages is what investors look for – they are skilled at identifying businesses with real growth potential, often before the founders themselves realise what a goldmine they're sitting on. While it's hard to establish future potential when you're low on cash and there are very few runs on the board, it's important that, as a founder, you take a brutally honest look at how your business is shaping up. If there is a genuine growth trajectory, your customers are happy and engaged, and you're receiving repeat business, then this is probably the time to dig deep and hold out on investor support. You want to avoid dilution at this critical stage in development.

My own experience with my chosen investor taught me an invaluable lesson in business, especially when I saw how they behaved towards me once their belt was squeezed. I watched on as they ran for cover, deflecting questions and escaping blame in the media. Inside their organisation, heads rolled, people left and a new administration was established. Most downturns in business signify a shift in the market or an issue that needs addressing, such as internal cultural problems, a change in consumer behaviour or the rise of a competitor. Pulling down the shutters and pretending there's nothing to see is the worst solution to a pattern of negative growth or declining customer satisfaction.

I was fortunate that the financial issues of my business partner didn't take my organisation down in the whitewash. To steady the business, my team and I pulled out every stop and moved into overdrive, working around the clock until we stood stronger than ever.

The aftermath of a crisis can play out in many different ways. I'm a problem-solver by nature, so when things get tough my mind moves into a hyper-operational mode. I break down all the issues and map them out according to time priorities and potential risks. I become task orientated and very detailed in my planning. Breaking down the issues into small, bite-sized pieces means that I can work through them in a highly systematic way.

In the first few days after being confronted with the reality of my business partner's turmoil, I made sure I focused on one piece of the puzzle at a time to ensure the issue in all its totality didn't cloud my judgement. My team followed suit, and each person took on a range of responsibilities to rebuild and reinstate stronger than before. We hired additional staff, invested in new technology and improved our digital systems. We developed a new rhythm and pulled in extra reserves to keep things moving forward.

The interrelationship between founders and investors can be complex. In my case, even as an experienced business person presenting a profitable entity, I was still on very unfair footing when I negotiated for equal terms in our partnership agreement. My investor was government backed, they had substance, and they had a high public profile. I was the owner of a four-year-old start-up. The shareholder agreement was written with the power weighted in their favour. The risk profile in the contract was drafted to assume that my business was far more likely to fail than theirs. My negotiation skills were well honed, but in hindsight I now see that I was too trusting and willing to accept terms that were not balanced. I put aside my usual levels of due diligence and legal advice, and I stepped into a financial relationship based on my perception of a large entity with a strong financial standing. My trust was misplaced.

## Not all storm clouds deliver rain

It's unavoidable that we'll all face people who try to take advantage of a good thing. In 2021 I supported three separate women founders who had all created great start-up businesses with real growth trajectory. All three were approached to see if they were interested in receiving investment in the first six to 18 months of their businesses. In all three cases, these founders were convinced to give up significant shareholdings in exchange for a modest amount of capital investment from an investor. The founders accepted these offers of financial support at a point when resources were limited, cash was low and the pressures of being a sole owner of a start-up business were being felt. In all cases, the investment promise didn't live up to the hype and they all found themselves working for a business where they had limited ownership, little to no decision-making power and no cash to grow.

I am saddened to see a recurring theme of investor bullying in early-stage businesses. There is a lack of maturity in our local investor market, meaning that too many people accept investor terms that are unrealistic or unethical. When I was establishing The Mind Lab and Tech Futures Lab, I spoke to multiple funds and investors about investment options. My question was simple: 'How many investments have you made in a women-founded business?' The answer? Not many. It was 2013 and I was seeking investment at a time when the start-up community was actively looking for businesses to invest in, yet I was unable to find a single fund that had invested significantly in a business founded exclusively by a woman.

Thankfully times have changed and there are now greater numbers of woman-founded businesses. Many funds now prioritise investment in woman-led organisations. Apparently in the tech world I am now classified as a pioneer for women in the sector. This is such a strange concept to me, as I still feel like a novice in so many situations. In 2017, I received a lifetime achievement award from the tech industry. I was 46. I remember thinking that I was far too young to be receiving an award for a lifetime of work. But even then I was just the third woman to be admitted into the New Zealand Hi-Tech Hall of Fame. I forget how new the technology sector is, but, more importantly, I forget how few women were in the sector two decades ago. Trailblazers seldom set out to cut new paths or to break down old doors. Necessity truly is the mother of invention and sacrifice.

I gave up looking for funders back in 2013 and decided to back myself. With the support of my family, I sold my two biggest assets – my home and my holiday home. I hired a team of the eight smartest people I knew and we moved into a shared working space. I didn't pay myself a dollar for the first two years but, with support from my family, we made things work. This was not the last time I sold my family home to provide the cash injection needed to build my business. Sometimes backing yourself is the best possible way to grow a business.

I have learned many things the hard way, by making decisions that I didn't fully comprehend or when I took on more than I could achieve, creating immense stress. As is the case for many people who develop their own business, there will be a time when an investment makes absolute sense if you are to truly scale beyond a small to medium enterprise. But having a partner or an investor goes much deeper than just finding someone who likes what you do.

When I advise my entrepreneurial graduate students on their start-up business ideas, we talk a lot about investors and investor motivations. Every founder has their own story to share about what worked and what didn't. My advice: once you have an investor your business is not entirely yours any more. It sounds obvious, but sometimes the excitement of having a backer can cloud the reason they're investing. Some investors will be great mentors and valuable contributors and others will be insensitive critics. Try to find out which one you're dealing with before you sign the agreement. In the end, an investor doesn't get returns until there is a liquidity event, which in simple terms means they need to sell at some stage, so don't be surprised by early talks of exit strategies.

I truly hope my early experiences as a female founder have long since been rectified, but I know old behaviours die hard.

In my life I have learned to weather storms. I decided long ago that no experience that was out of my control would be my undoing. I have always been pragmatic and I believe that all things happen for a reason. When I look back at the investment I took on for my business, I don't regret what happened as it gave me renewed confidence in myself and my team. The biggest achievements of our organisation have occurred since the partnership ended. My team has stood by me every step of the way, as we took our foot off the brake and focused on leading by doing. It turned out that the unexpected freedom to operate meant we could move faster and be more deliberate in our actions.

If you are at the start of your entrepreneurial journey, I encourage you to plan for success but be prepared for the unexpected. Changing the world takes people who are willing to risk it all, and good ideas will always flourish if you believe in what you're doing.

Sometimes I wish I could wake up and not have the weight of responsibility on my shoulders, but these moments are fleeting. I now know more than ever that not all storm clouds deliver rain. Sometimes you just need to pack your umbrella and carry on. Sunshine is always just round the corner.

## CHAPTER 16

# Imposter syndrome

## Give up on perfection – it doesn't exist

### Do one brave thing at a time

Some days I have a feeling of delight that takes me by surprise. It's like a gush of love for life and living. Sometimes it's based on a particular environment, a person, an experience or a memory, but at other times it just emerges out of nowhere. It's as though my mind has decided to send a dose of endorphins to my brain to remind me of how great life can be. We all have our happy places, with ties to the people or experiences we most value.

Then there are days when I lose perspective of all the good things in life and the future feels heavy, unapproachable and intimidating. I grew up thinking that only some people have these days. I thought that some people had mental-health challenges and some didn't. It took me years to truly understand how misinformed this assumption was. Everyone has bad days. I have them, my family have them, my colleagues have them. Whether the people we care about are diagnosed with mental-health challenges or grappling with anxiety caused by unexpected circumstances, our role as good leaders, parents and friends is to support them.

True leaders can connect with their teams using respect, trust and empathy. They display a strong sense of self and remain grounded even when they feel fearful. They can also shift their focus and priorities when members of their family or team need support or encouragement. They don't claim to have the answers, but are instead open to listening and letting others be heard and understood. These leaders are comfortable showing their vulnerabilities when things are not going well, they're willing to share their authentic selves, and they encourage others to do the same.

Not all days are alike. Our energy can change significantly from day to day, and the way we 'show up' on any given day is often determined by conditions well outside our control. If you work in health or education, chances are you will have some understanding of neuroplasticity and how our brains adapt to change. I think of my brain as a customised map of the outside world. The more experiences and inputs my brain has, the more reserves it has to call upon when I'm presented with challenging or new experiences. Thanks to significant advances in neurology, we now know how and when the brain best responds to learning and change. Contrary to what many people believe, when something difficult or challenging occurs in our lives, our brains develop an intense focus, stimulating specific neurons to be more active and more open.

Young brains are much more responsive to learning, and in the earliest years of our lives we are capable of comprehending multiple new things simultaneously, including multiple languages and new subject material. Even learning physical activities, sports and manual tasks is undertaken with very little conscious thought. Through these early years, it can be beneficial to experience many new or unfamiliar situations as these experiences tag specific neurons and get them prepared for difficult situations that may occur later in life. But even with a basic understanding of how the brain works, and knowing how I personally respond to different situations, I can still find myself feeling like I'm masquerading as a leader in so many different environments.

The feeling of being out of your depth or out of control is common. It is very rare to find a person who doesn't harbour the fear they're not good enough. They might think they aren't good enough to lead, to contribute, to share or even to hold the role they're currently in. But measuring competency is very subjective. We use this term frequently in education to determine whether a student has developed the comprehension needed to be able to apply their knowledge with credible understanding. In our own evaluation of our competency, we can be extraordinarily harsh. We are often our own worst critics.

'Fake it until you make it' is often shared as sound advice for people stepping into new territory or new situations. When I hear this term I think of the people I've met in my life who had a swagger and confidence that I've never felt. My advice: never pretend to be someone you are not. Do one brave thing at a time, take one baby step each day, and let your confidence build as you see your capabilities grow.

Even the most self-assured person can relate to the concept of imposter syndrome. It's the feeling of doubt that creeps in during self-reflection, or when a passing comment rattles your confidence. I'm very familiar with the feeling of imposter syndrome, but I'm uneasy about the term – it has pretty negative connotations. An imposter is someone who doesn't belong, someone excluded. The insinuation is that imposters are people excluded for prejudicial reasons, including race, gender or age. It's important that we understand systemic bias, privilege and racism as very real issues, as well as Eurocentric or heteronormative views that make some people feel excluded regardless of their rights. 'Imposter syndrome' captures a much broader issue of not feeling worthy or feeling redundant in an environment. Many people who feel this sense of inadequacy worry they're going to be found out as frauds, even when they have all the skills and credentials for a role, a company or a community.

This doubt can play out time and time again and it sometimes causes people to disengage from life or to choose less challenging or fulfilling roles, all because of their assumption that they may not be good enough, especially in comparison to others. Even when a person has all the obvious signs of success, including qualifications or industry recognition, the feeling of intellectual phoniness is a very real issue.

In my graduate classes, I often speak with senior executives who legitimately question how they became qualified, as though their previous studies and academic successes were somehow a stroke of good luck or trickery. When adult students enter formal studies after a long absence, they often compare their fear of learning with their fear of being asked to drive an initiative that they don't feel they have the skills or capacity to handle. Most people experience some level of self-doubt when facing a new challenge, but when this doubt becomes a real fear of being found out, the thought pattern can be very detrimental to personal development.

## Perfection is not a destination

There is one common character type within organisations that is crippling: the adult perfectionist who has always been a super achiever. When these adults become students in my institute, they're typically in their forties and they have a deep-seated fear of someone judging their performance. Sometimes they obsess over details or become overly concerned about assessments or presentations. Our role in these situations is to reassure them that perfection doesn't exist, in learning or in life. Knowledge is permeable and fluid, and even the most sound theories change over time as new information comes to light.

By the time these students finish their studies they have generally relaxed and accepted the fact that perfection is not a destination, and the journey of learning, unlearning and relearning is a critical part of studying.

The overarching theme of self-doubt is that people underestimate their abilities even when there is tangible evidence to the contrary. Society often focuses on the very highest achievers instead of the everyday people who are the backbone of economies and communities. If we decide only the people who sit on the highest pedestals of success are symbols of accomplishment, we miss noticing some of the strongest and most competent people around us.

We are surrounded by stories, in the media, in literature, on TV and in film, that show all great leaders as ruling from the front. The media loves dominant, extroverted or charismatic leaders, and popular culture paints a narrow picture of success that mostly hasn't changed for many decades. As a female leader, I have regularly fought my own perception of what a leader should be. In my interactions with esteemed leaders I have seen courageous, bold people who portray strength like a badge of honour. Bursting self-confidence is foreign to me and I have often felt inferior when in the company of charismatic leaders.

I attribute a lot of my doubt to my experience working with technologists, innovators and developers for so many years. The first few decades of my career were spent with people who were often anti-establishment and who lived in defiance of the traditional characteristics of business leaders. These communities were far less hierarchical and they only loosely adhered to defined roles and responsibilities. Typically, they focused on what they did well and what they loved, with little consideration for what the system said. It has been fascinating to watch the tech industry come into its own, moving away from being seen as the domain of geeks and boffins, to become the field for aspirational entrepreneurs of the future. The industry has lost its reputation as being a fringe contributor to the economy, and it is now viewed as one of our most valued sectors, with the greatest potential to transform our economy. When I look around tech networking events, I am ecstatic to see larger numbers of women and a diverse workforce bringing their expertise and different perspectives.

The rise of technology in business, and our reliance on software and hardware as the tools of the trade, has led to the dramatic movement of the people who write code and build integrations from the edges of business into the heart of enterprises. Our children and grandchildren will see technology through a different lens. Their world will be shaped by code, enabling them to operate without the constraints we have today.

Maybe this will be the era that imposter syndrome ceases to exist, as we all deepen our appreciation of the benefits of diversity and the advantages of building a work community based on a broad set of skills, backgrounds and experience. If our future workplaces are less about 'fitting in' and more about belonging, maybe we'll embrace new and unfamiliar ways without trepidation.

I hope we come to define leaders with a broader, different view. Perhaps that'll be when we will truly see change being made on the basis of inclusiveness, equity and the understanding of many, not a few. I am encouraged by Generation Z and millennials, who are breaking the rules of the past decades to create a workforce of the future, one that represents a vision of the world they want to be part of.

**CHAPTER 17**

# Power struggles

Keep your eye on the prize

## Old enemies, new tricks

People never fail to astound me. It doesn't seem like a high threshold to expect common courtesy and a level of relative consistency in behaviour from someone. But we all know that life is inconsistent, and motivations can vary greatly from one person to the next. A single action can undo a lifetime of hard work, and it's all too familiar when someone influential with a curated public image is revealed to have behaved indulgently or corruptly. When someone we once admired falls from grace and their life unravels, it's a headline grabber.

I have witnessed some incredibly disrespectful actions. I have been privy to conversations between people that show ignorance, arrogance, racism or narcissistic tendencies. I have watched leaders take great joy in stripping down their employees and belittling others for human error, physical appearance and even dress sense. I have worked for battle-ready, aggressive alpha leaders who have had to win at all costs. We all face bullies and their impact is unavoidable.

A close friend who has spent her life working in advertising recently sent me an article on the culture of the advertising industry that reflected some of her first-hand experiences. It painted a detailed picture of a highly volatile and manipulative work environment that operated on fear. It is easy to control another person with fear – and so destructive. You can threaten their job, threaten blacklisting them from the sector, threaten limiting their salary advancement or relegating them to secondary roles as a form of punishment. Fear has a silencing effect too. You might fear being labelled a prude, naysayer or killjoy if you raise your concerns, or if you choose not to participate in certain workplace antics.

It has, thankfully, become harder for powerful people to hide their exploitation of those who work for them. Whistle-blower processes, as well as greater caution and awareness of the conditions in which power imbalances thrive, have become board-level issues. But manipulation is everywhere. I dream of a day when people never experience unwanted advances or innuendo from colleagues. And when career advancement is not determined by the colour of your skin or where you went to school. The power and hierarchies of the past are outdated and yet they survive despite all the efforts that have claimed to break them down. I have worked with many businesses that talk about the need to employ and support younger or more culturally diverse employees. But talking is of no value if these employees look up to the executive team or the board of directors and see no diversity.

Change takes time, but does it really have to take this long? With the added threats of online bullying, anonymous harassment and invisible tormentors, it can be hard to tell if we are really moving forward. Have we just moved the issue to a space where there are fewer controls and almost no ability to apprehend the perpetrators?

The article my friend sent me closed with a paragraph from the author saying that, as a 36-year-old woman sharing her views of misogyny on Twitter, she has faced unsolicited advances, dick pics, rape threats and death threats. When I was younger and the recipient of unwanted advances, I could see my tormentors and their actions were tangible. I was able to react in person. Online tormentors and anonymous written attacks via social media have reached fever pitch. Too many people are relentlessly bullied for speaking out against dated systems and behaviours that need addressing. Online attackers are able to target someone through multiple channels at any time, reaching into the safety of someone's home, all under the cloak of anonymity. The fear this causes can be paralysing.

As a young person I believed that corrupt people were mostly only powerful in packs: the drunken team, the misogynist executive group, the radical collective. But this is no longer true. A single person can now have a significant impact on another without ever having to face them. It's hard to isolate a bully and disable their power if you don't know who or where they are. I hope that one day we'll treat online intimidation the same way we treat in-person oppressors. Blocking someone online is the wrong tool for a complex issue. Social networks need to take responsibility for curbing online harassment. Preventing online trolls and attackers, and protecting people's privacy, should be given the highest priority.

## Culture versus control

All generations have experienced the classic aggressor boss who takes great joy in making members of their organisation break under pressure. I have been in boardrooms where the tension was so intense you could've cut the air with a knife. I have also led strategy sessions where no one spoke a word until the chief executive left the room. You can't tell someone's a tormentor just by what they look like or what others say about them. We all learn to become attuned to the characteristics that indicate deviant or oppressive behaviour.

I have lived through two distinct models of business leadership: the hierarchical model, in which decisions are pushed from the top down through the organisation, and the flat structure, in which decisions are developed and fed in from all parts of the organisation and initiatives can be created without the need for buy-in from the top table.

It's naive to think that traditional organisational hierarchies can provide solutions to the challenges of the twenty-first century. Yet many leaders today are challenged by the open and increasingly egalitarian expectations of their employees. Today's workplaces come with certain expectations about the need to quash unacceptable practices, but it is not unusual for a traditional leader to manipulate or bypass agreed processes to re-establish old behaviours in a display of leadership disobedience. This behaviour has been particularly apparent in businesses looking to re-establish the controls of a pre-Covid-19 world. I have seen executives overriding the directive of a company to reinforce expectations of their team's working hours and location. I have also seen flexibility being reined in as a form of control and in order to reinstate old ways. Where there is change, there will be tension. For people who have always dominated directives to suit their views, it's uncomfortable to have to adopt new learnings and this can lead to power plays.

I liken these responses to a person entering a paddock with a bull standing in the far corner. In the initial period of change the person has entered the paddock with the bull and there is interest and observation, but very little concern. Phase one is a quiet standoff: both parties continue to do their own thing, and neither is particularly interested in the other. When the person moves forward into the next phase, the bull feels threatened and puffs up to change their physical stance and show power and intimidation. If this action fails to deter the approach, the bull will eventually charge. The charging bull is the person fighting to retain their power in a world that is changing around them. These individuals can make lots of noise and the occasional threat, but as more and more people step towards them, their power lessens.

It will take time to transition from traditional hierarchical structures to more diverse and agile models. However, we can already see the changes and benefits as the voice of change grows louder, calling out dated behaviours and controls.

Are you the bull resisting change and progress? Or you are the person wanting to drive progress through a sea of resistance? Either way, we're all on a journey of change. Every new action we put in place has the potential to be the circuit breaker needed to reset a system or to re-establish the direction you're heading.

If you find yourself following the same path, protecting the same actions or having the same conversations, it's important to understand that the power to improve things sits with you. If you overthink and deliberate for too long, your energy and forward momentum will dwindle and your motivation will diminish. If you actively push the go button on making changes in your life, you'll fire up the key cognitive functions needed to move beyond what researchers call a 'mental impasse', or the barrier that needs to be overcome to untangle a problem.

Committing to a different outcome or a new action kickstarts the inflexible part of your brain, unlocking your ability to free your mind from known behaviours. Putting your brain into a receptive mode is a form of liberation, as you switch off the control mode and think more freely.

Every organisation has its own underlying culture. In the same way that many families develop regular rituals and routines, workplace cultures are guided by unspoken assumptions about priorities and actions. Many of the cultural nuances within an organisation are intangible and difficult to articulate or see until you're deeply immersed in the business. A strong business culture is one of the most important ways to connect people to the work they do. If a business has a misaligned or weak culture, employees will find themselves confused about where they fit and unsure how to connect with other team members.

I have witnessed the bounce effect a number of times in my career, when a new member literally bounces out the door shortly after beginning their role because of a misalignment of culture and values. Each time the person felt isolated by their inability to assimilate into the business's operations. In many ways, leaving an organisation shortly after starting because of misaligned values or practices is a very astute call. It's similar to cutting short a first date because of a lack of chemistry – sometimes the intangible things have the most significant impact on how you feel.

If you're working in an organisation committed to transformational change, the first piece of the puzzle is to focus on creating a culture that moves away from rewarding consistency, predictability and the status quo. Adaptable organisations are highly receptive to change and make a visible commitment to flexibility; the command-and-control structures of the past feel out of place.

When I think of my friend's experiences in the heyday of advertising, I wonder why we ever tolerated business leaders whose behaviour would've been inappropriate in a personal setting. For decades the media celebrated as idols the high-profile business leaders who behaved inappropriately – is it possible that this created a level of tolerance for such behaviour? People we once held in high regard now face legal cases detailing their domination, abuse and power. Is corrupt behaviour by the powerful a part of life that we can't avoid? Or is this the time in history when changing expectations, greater accountability and demands for transparency will expose the last of the domineering alpha leaders for what they really are?

Intimidation has no place in business or in life. Coercion, persuasion, inducements and manipulation have been part of business since the first days of trade. We have to decide whether we'll continue to buy into these influences or make a stand against them. The powers of the past may be diminishing, but new forms of control are already emerging in their place. Will we adopt these new strongholds of domination or resist them?

The challenges we face and the problems we must solve have many common characteristics packaged differently. If you find that you've lost perspective of what is truly important, it may be that you need to look at the issue from another angle. Linear vision is the brain's way of narrowing down an issue, but sometimes it clouds our ability to see the full picture of what needs to happen.

## Stand your ground

One of the greatest challenges you can face as an employee is a lack of career progression. For example, you might work in an organisation that has overlooked you for a promotion in favour of someone who is more openly ambitious. The first step you can take to address this issue is to view it as an opportunity to improve and learn. Take a proactive approach: compile a list of the reasons you were a suitable candidate, and include the skills you've developed during your employment. Next, ask to meet with your manager and be explicit about what the meeting is for, framing it as a development opportunity to talk about your career goals. Sometimes bringing your aspirations to the table helps – your manager may not have seen your ambition to grow and take on greater responsibility. This is not uncommon when an individual is highly competent in one specific role and has made themselves almost indispensable because of their specialised skills and high-level capabilities. In this scenario, your employer may be consciously or unconsciously keeping you in a specific function because they haven't identified or developed your replacement. You could even help them identify a suitable replacement or offer to help develop another member of the team, and show your manager your growth potential.

Whatever the issue you're hoping to address, it's important to find the right time and setting to talk through your concerns. Set a time and an agenda for a discussion and outline the rules of engagement so that all parties are free to express their views. In business, as in friendships and relationships, facilitating an open dialogue with clear intentions, free of emotion and implication, will help resolve issues in a far more constructive way than 'unofficial' conversations from the sidelines.

Very few people are truly comfortable sharing what they think when addressing an issue, particularly if other people are involved. Whether your goal is to break through as a leader, change your company culture, remove long-standing divides or create new pathways to develop innovations, it's important that you emphasise the need for open communication channels. Many of the most successful companies I have worked with have an entrepreneurial spirit. Employees are encouraged to collaborate and when problems are brought to the table they're seen as an opportunity to improve or resolve underlying issues.

Our influence in a working environment is often tied directly to our relationships with others. These relationships should be built on trust and open communication, not the tenuous connections some people build as a means of self-promotion and self-aggrandisement.

Some people in the workplace make it difficult to solve problems or try to slow processes down for no obvious reason beyond making themselves look important. I have seen this characteristic enough times to know these individuals often also undermine others.

Once bitten, twice shy is a very real reaction. If you are trying to resolve an issue with a person who's inconsistent and unpredictable, particularly if they're friendly and accommodating on some occasions but verbally abusive on others, there is really only one solution: get them out. People like this can jeopardise more than work relationships – they can cause havoc that has far-reaching consequences. They allow themselves to become mired in anger, or impeded by their sense of inaction, while claiming to be disconnected from the community. In time they will function as a destructive lone operator.

If someone is belligerent or overly combative, and you're unable to change their negative influence on you, don't waste any more valuable energy on them. Find a way out. Focus on your happy future, a place where you can be inspired every day.

## Actions speak louder than words

Navigating the workplace can be challenging. Work cultures are nuanced, and individuals or outdated processes can have a significant effect on a business's ability to thrive. Whether a work culture thrives or not will often be the result of which actions are allowed and which are called out. Structures in the workplace have been slow evolving over many years. Businesses that were formed recently are far more likely to reflect contemporary work practices, whereas long-established organisations will often carry legacy practices that are overlooked because they're so entrenched in the way the business functions. Identifying practices that no longer work should be part of an ongoing review of systems. No change happens without an initiator or a catalyst, and the best catalyst is one that has been discovered proactively rather than through failure.

If you want to achieve success, focus on the people around you who do not waste time complaining or indulging in the negativity of others. If you don't like something in your work or life, find a way to change it. Take charge of the situation and find a workaround or a solution. In the end, you have one life and it's entirely reasonable to want to make it as rewarding as it can be.

## CHAPTER 18

# Becoming an entrepreneur

## Stay committed

### The journey is bitter and sweet

Successful people do the things they love. Many characteristics are commonly attributed to successful people, but in most cases success comes down a person's ability to create positive behaviours that align their interests with their work, and their ability to dream. Entrepreneurs often take these skills and push them even further, propelling themselves and those around them to new heights.

Entrepreneurs are self-starters who seldom linger in their comfort zone. They constantly strive towards something and never allow inertia to set in. Successful entrepreneurs know that time is a limited and valuable resource, so their focus is on keeping things moving forward. The successful entrepreneur feels comfortable without routine, and accepts that there is never truly a day when they're not thinking about how to improve things or push boundaries.

The difference between an entrepreneur and a person who aspires to run their own business is scale, time and impact. Entrepreneurs are oriented to growth and expansion. They often focus on innovation and ideas that haven't been done before. They thrive (or die) on innovation, adaptation and implementation of a technology, product or service. Entrepreneurs generally move quickly, and are strongly motivated to create an impact. For some, this will be socially driven or formed by a desire to improve access to a product or service, while others will be driven by a desire to create wealth. Business owners are more likely to establish a business in a field or area where there is known demand, and where there is greater similarity to other competitors in their sector.

There is conflicting evidence as to whether entrepreneurs can be created with the right stimulus or settings – they might realise that there is a significant unmet need in the market, or they might adapt out of necessity due to a job loss or relocation. I like to think that everyone has the potential to be an entrepreneur, but most people just don't make the leap into the unknown. Once a person has launched one successful business, they are much more likely to go on to start another successful organisation. There is a formula to success – it starts with a great idea, a lot of hard work and creativity, and a number of key ingredients that can be applied to almost any business idea. But the uncertainty of going from an idea to a fully-fledged business is not for everyone.

From a young age I quietly rebelled against the idea of a traditional career path. Like other entrepreneurs I know, I have a real passion for doing something new, especially if it results in creating something better than what is readily available. While I had early entrepreneurial aspirations from the time I first ran my family's roadside berry store, I dabbled as a sole trader in the years after my return to New Zealand from Europe before I found the confidence to commit to building an enterprise with scale.

My first business was a marketing consultancy, my second an interactive company focused on computer vision and immersive interactions. But I haven't always owned or operated businesses in technology and education. When my children were in primary school, I wanted to be closer to them so I took a sabbatical from my career in technology education and followed my love of food and cooking. I established a rural food store and cafe, close to where I lived on our family lifestyle block. I fitted out an existing shed and added a refrigerated shipping container, a kitchen, a cafe area, bathrooms and decor reminiscent of a European food market. The biggest investment in this business was my commitment to provide high-quality fruit and vegetables, presented in large cane baskets and rustic boxes. This decision required me to get out of bed at 3.30 am three times a week, get into my pickup truck and head out to buy produce from the local trading market. It seems ironic now that my childhood experience running a rural produce store somehow became part of my life again as an adult. What astounds me most is that, over the 11 months I owned the food store, I never once really thought about the connection between my childhood experience and how I was now replicating it 20 years later in a different part of the country.

Running this food store was hard. Really hard. In ways that are so different from running a knowledge-based business. My business attire was replaced by jeans and sweaters, and through the winter months I literally piled on layer after layer of clothing to ward off the bitter cold from the concrete floor at the market as I wheeled my trolley between sellers. Three times a week I arrived at my food store well before sunrise and I lugged multiple crates filled with vegetables to the chiller. Over time I could lift two fully laden crates of pumpkins above my head to stack them. My physical fitness had never been better but my enjoyment of work diminished significantly with the grind of working so many hours alone.

While I supplemented peak trading times by hiring casual staff, they were typically young and rostered on for the busy periods, when we would all be busy attending to the needs of the customers. My only full-time staff member was my chef, but she was tucked away in the kitchen while I ran front of house. I found the isolation from people and the absence of interesting conversations the hardest part of the process. The financial returns were inconsistent, and at times the relentlessness and monotony of the work was heartbreaking. To try to make ends meet, I worked more hours without staff to keep costs down. Seven days a week I would work morning until night. My children were in much closer proximity and they would come to the food store at the end of the day and on weekends, but my disconnect from education, technology and bold discussions about the future left me feeling less motivated than I had ever been.

By the time the first anniversary of the business was in sight, I was faced with two options. I could invest further to grow the business, expanding my offering to include online, and broaden my products, or I could sell. I sold. Truth is, I started the business because I wanted to be nearer to my children, but the reality was I had lost confidence in myself. I was doing something that I didn't have a passion for and I felt drained at the end of every day. I needed to get back to education and what I really loved.

When 2013 came around I was a mission-driven entrepreneur, committed to building learning institutes for adults who were looking to deepen their understanding of the technological and societal levers of change. At 40, when I undertook my master's studies as an adult learner, I realised that there were very few flexible options to learn as a mature adult. My hunt for a programme that would put me with a group of professionals led me to study at the University of Melbourne, where I discovered the benefits of a residential-based part-time programme that could work around my busy life.

This one insight led me on a path of research and discovery, and eventually led to the development of The Mind Lab and, later, Tech Futures Lab. Both were inspired by and designed to meet the reskilling needs of busy adults. Like many entrepreneurs, I have always been an early adopter of technology and I understand the importance of innovation driven by investment in research and development.

Most entrepreneurs focus on the customer, the unmet needs of the market and areas where substantial improvements can be made. Those entrepreneurs who repeatedly create successful businesses have a gift for seeing emerging market opportunities, and for delivering a service or product that outperforms or is more affordable than those of competitors.

A real strength of entrepreneurs is their ability to accept constructive criticism, and to use feedback to continuously improve their products or services. They have a heightened sense of ownership, due to their significant skin in the game, making them very responsive to negative feedback. Success or failure of an idea generally falls squarely on a founder's shoulders, and they often have significant money tied up in their business's success, so there is a direct correlation between meeting market need and the sustainability of the business.

It could be that my views are skewed by my personal network, but the majority of entrepreneurs I know are also introverted, and prefer to work in the establishment phase on their own. I haven't yet decided if an entrepreneur's decision to work in isolation during the start-up stage is to minimise risk or to enable them to focus fully on the business without distraction. They might hire staff or seek advisors, but they will often take on the big initial decisions on their own, before recruiting highly skilled individuals who are aligned with the business's vision.

The last decade has seen the rise of businesses underpinned by technology that enables rapid growth, the use and collection of data, and the deployment of platforms to reach new markets. Entrepreneurs who operate in this space often disrupt analogue, traditional business by reimagining it through a technological lens. These entrepreneurs recognise that analogue business systems, traditional paper-based processes and one-to-one business models have mostly reached their use-by date.

We have long since exited the industrial era, when all work was physical, labour-intensive and focused on physical outputs. Today it is our minds, and our comprehension and application of new knowledge and technology, that do most of the heavy lifting. The tools of today are designed to support and integrate with technological systems and interfaces to get the job done – faster, better and with more consistent results. In future decades from now, our businesses will operate on integrated systems, hardware and software, and our job is to make sound strategic decisions informed by contemporary best practice. Operating on outdated knowledge is like operating on an outdated computer or software that is no longer supported. If the knowledge we hold has been superseded by something better, we need to upgrade. Running at half speed or on partial understanding can do more than just reduce financial returns; it makes organisations less attractive to the next generation of employees and less responsive to customer expectations. Regardless of which sector you work in, you need to be open to change – we all do. The next five to ten years will see even further digitalisation of business systems and processes. To stay relevant, employed and in control of your future you will have to step into the unknown and be open to change.

## A few words of advice

If you are a first-time entrepreneur, the most important piece of advice I can give is to establish your cash-flow needs before you get going. Regardless of whether you're creating a slow-burning side hustle working from your garage or you're starting your business with a team of people, you need to know how long your financial runway will last if you have no income. Everyone assumes money will flow in faster than it does and sales will increase more rapidly than they do. I have seen many great business ideas fail because the money simply ran out before the business ever really got going.

Secondly, your first hire should be the most skilled person you can find who you can't really afford. You are far better to pay someone who brings essential expertise to the business than to pay yourself well. Going it alone is a very lonely place to be. The addition of a seasoned expert brings an amplifying effect. One plus one, in this case, equals three. Grow slowly at first. Deploy every cost-saving digital tool you can and make your business operate autonomously using simple tools such as autoresponders for enquiries or e-commerce sites for sales. But, when it comes to your first employee, go big. Nothing will move the dial faster than someone who knows what they're doing.

Thirdly, build your brand. Before people buy on the reputation of a new company, they have to buy on the brand promise. Make sure your brand is developed to cut through the noise and the competition. You don't have to be the biggest to be successful, but you do need to be visible and memorable.

There are many benefits to founding and running your own high-growth business. One lesser-known benefit is that the journey of running your own business is not ageist. People who start businesses later in life are generally much more successful than those who start their entrepreneurial dream in their twenties and thirties. I suspect this is mostly because as we age our priorities change, and we have a better understanding of what makes us happiest. A business you create later in life is far more likely to be based on skills you already have and in an area where you have existing expertise and experience. Having higher levels of cash reserves and assets to leverage also helps with the cash-flow challenges through the start-up period.

If you're thinking about branching out of employment to start your own venture, make sure you have an idea that you believe in so much that you would fall on your sword just to bring it to life. If you are only lukewarm on your idea, or if you are buying an existing business and you lack passion for what the business does, you will never feel the joy of being your own boss. There is no room for ambivalence when it comes to starting a business. You are 110 per cent in, or you'll fail before the first year of trading rolls round. However, don't misinterpret your fear and doubt as a justification for not proceeding with your own business. Apprehension and unease are a sign that you care. Use these emotions to fuel your drive to do well.

One of the biggest myths about becoming your own boss is that you will never have to deal with the complexities and frustrations of being an employee. The truth is the things that were time consuming as an employee are amplified as an employer. Human-resource issues, budgeting, office politics, staff welfare, ineffective marketing campaigns and taxes all become your problem, even if you employ people to do these roles. Working for yourself is still work. It requires time, passion, energy, planning and risk.

It is commonly said that only one in ten business start-ups are successful enough to make it to the three-year mark. But this shouldn't stop anyone from trying. Focus on what success looks like, and what it will enable you to do. Visualise the time when your business is thriving and making a real difference. Think beyond the fear and imagine what your future creation will look like when you achieve your goals. The fear of failure will never completely disappear. But your belief in what you can achieve will push you to achieve even more.

# Would've, could've, should've

## Everything is possible

What we have done or achieved in the past is a place of reference and reflection. It is not a place of residency. I believe that your brain has an incredible power to make all the right decisions to get you to where you want to be. Your role is to let your brain know the destination.

My career has spanned more than a quarter of a century. My time and priority has mostly been focused on people's ability to learn, evolve and respond to change. Most of the conversations I'm part of relate to technology and adaptation, and the catalysts required for a person to change their path or deviate from where they're heading.

Experience shows we all have a threshold that enables us to support or resist unfamiliar things or activities that we have never done before. The line between stepping into the unknown and holding on to the familiar is very personal and varies significantly from one person to another. A person who has been told they have weeks left to live is massively motivated to try anything to delay their death sentence. Likewise, a person who falls in love and yearns to be at the side of their loved one will make drastic life changes to stay together.

People respond to information in different ways. My neighbour at the start of this book decided he was too old to learn new skills, even with notice of his job redundancy. People limit their careers by believing that they are less capable than the person next to them. Others miss the opportunity to recognise the untapped talent around them because they can't see beyond the people who look just like themselves. Most people keep their goals and aspirations hidden because they fear they may not be achieved. Others will walk over anyone in their way to achieve their goals with no consideration for the harm they might inflict.

Whether by good design or total coincidence, I discovered that my strongest mechanism for following through with my commitments is to share my plans with others. I don't mean sharing for the sake of exchanging ideas and information, but sharing with the explicit intention of telling people what I plan to do. This might involve informing my staff of a significant new project tied to an ambitious timeframe, or announcing a personal goal in front of a large gathering of family and friends. Sometimes I have even made a public commitment through a media interview. Regardless of the method, I have found that making my goals widely known to others compels me to follow through. This public sharing process works well for me. By stating my intentions I become hyper-focused and deliberate.

I suspect we all know people who require a lot of personal praise and accolades before they attempt something new. This behaviour is common in people who often talk about the things that they are going to do, but appear to do very little to actually realise their goal. This may be a colleague who has talked about running a marathon for years and finally informs you they are actually going to do it. If the response they receive is underwhelming and doesn't come with significant admiration, they'll often backtrack and find reasons not to follow through. If you want to make changes to your life that put you on the path to a more fulfilling future, you will need to become your own best champion. You can seek advice, build a support network and tell everyone your plans, but the only person who will make your dream happen is you.

We all like to be acknowledged for doing something that others think is challenging. But when you are making sustained changes and improvements in your life you need to build personal resilience as a form of reinforcement for when things don't go entirely to plan. Humans are driven by all sorts of motivations and needs. Look back across your life and think of a time you made a positive change. What steps did you take that supported you to stay with the programme?

Some people need to make a public pledge or come up with consequences to make a change. This theory is the basis of many weight-loss programmes. By stating a weight-loss goal to a group of people, and by sharing data on weekly weigh-ins, people make the change happen. This is also the model of many charities that run campaigns based on supporters abstaining from certain vices, such as alcohol or technology, for a set period of time. The motivation in these scenarios is the fear of letting the charity down and having to tell your friends that the goal was not achieved. The combination of the public pledge and reward-based incentive leads people to follow through on their commitments.

Then there are the people who make drastic changes for the love of a person and the desire to make someone else happy. This might include moving cities, taking up dancing, learning a new language or developing the skills for a more lucrative career. Love is a very powerful motivator – perhaps the most powerful of them all.

Change for the sake of improving future benefits is tough. This is the type of change needed for people to put money towards their retirement savings, or developing skills for the future, or staying fit for long-term health and longevity. We all downplay the likelihood of major risk events occurring in our world. We assume our good health will continue, and our financial situation will improve as we age. We imagine that our job prospects will always be strong and the people around us will be safe. But our futures are determined by many factors outside our control. We can be sideswiped by events that have never come on to our radar, or circumstances that were unimaginable.

Life is complex and it's filled with uncertainty. We will never know what would have happened if we had chosen a different path or if we had made a different decision. If some of the hardest chapters in my journey had not occurred, would I still have developed the ability to dig deep and forge on when things got tough? Have my lived experiences been curated by my heart or my mind? Am I merely a product of circumstance? I'll never know.

I have spent the better part of my life so far trying to understand why some people don't embrace change even when they know their future depends on it. Why do we rationalise fear when we don't try to rationalise love? I hope that as you've read this book you've been able to see change for the benefits it brings and accept that embracing the unknown is an integral part of living and life. Open-mindedness is a conscious process that we can all embrace if we're willing to accept that doing things differently is part of learning and self-improvement.

Every person sees life through a unique lens. We all experience different inputs and influences, and we all have the ability to examine how we show up or respond to the world around us. The difficulties of life are very real, and there's no known way to mitigate all of the challenges that we'll have to navigate during our time on this earth.

Organisations, like communities, have their own ecosystems, and each system has its own culture and attitude towards progress, innovation and adaptation. If you are leading a team, a business or a grassroots initiative, it is important to encourage innovation and receptivity to embark on a journey of development and change. Uncertainty or forging ahead with no plan typically comes with negative consequences.

## Saying yes

When I was 35, I made one very specific commitment to myself that has had a greater positive impact on my life and my journey than all others. I made the decision to live my life filled with everything it delivered. This started with a very public commitment to say yes to everything that was asked of me. My rules were simple. Providing the request was ethical and I was able to fit it into my diary, I would say yes. I started my commitment on a day that has no other particular significance. There was no big flash of inspiration or moment of clarity that preceded the decision. It was simply a conscious decision to live life to its fullest and to ensure I didn't miss opportunities or have moments of regret.

My commitment was ring-fenced to a 15-year period between the ages of 35 and 50. At 35, I found it hard to even imagine myself being 50. I had no idea how much would change in the 15 years between those two moments in time. At 35 my biggest focus was raising my children, being a great mother and wife, and balancing my career while maintaining the ever-elusive work–life balance. It was impossible for me to imagine that in just 15 years my children would be in their twenties and living away from home with amazing partners and big careers ahead of them. I didn't for one second imagine I would be the founder and chief executive of two organisations with over a hundred staff and thousands of adult students, or that I would be part of a locked-down world forced to change as a matter of survival against a pandemic.

I should also mention that at 35 I had never spoken at a conference, researched a cause or rallied support for reform.

When I informed everyone I would say yes to all reasonable requests, the world around me changed. Overnight.

I soon discovered that I had a role championing women in technology and another advocating for education progress. I found myself speaking about emerging technology and the future of work at events, and presenting sound arguments for the increased benefits of increasing the number of women in tech and in senior roles in business and governance. Soon my boardroom conversations became keynote engagements at conferences, then sponsored talks offshore, and eventually presentations at some of the biggest speaking events in the world. The momentum snowballed and by the time I was 45 I was speaking at one or two conferences per week. The shy girl from the farm grew a quiet confidence.

While many of the most influential and beneficial experiences of my life came about because of my commitment to saying yes, not all of them panned out as I thought they would. One particular time I was asked to speak at a large CEO event in Amsterdam. It was a one-day conference and I would be the first speaker after the conference lunch. When they asked if I could fly to the Netherlands, I checked my diary and saw a small window of opportunity between existing commitments that would mean I'd have to fly to Europe and back within three days. I planned my journey so that my flight would arrive in the Netherlands a mere three hours before showtime.

I left New Zealand in the middle of summer to head into the depths of snow and winter. Under my make-up I was also hiding a significant shiner, with a black eye, a broken cheekbone, and deep purple bruising from my forehead to the bottom of my neck, after tripping over a friend's dog at full running speed. But my commitment is my promise, so decked out in my winter woollies I boarded my 28-hour flight to Amsterdam. On arrival at Schiphol

Airport I checked into an airport hotel and I was soon on my way to the venue, a beautifully appointed golf-club retreat with a conference room that looked directly out to a field covered in thick snow that claimed all features in the surrounding landscape.

I arrived just as the conference delegates were breaking for lunch. I was notified that the kitchen was running well behind schedule and the lunch would delay my talk for up to an hour. The conference organiser cancelled the final speaker of the day, who was due to speak immediately after me, to ensure that the attendees could leave the conference on time.

The extra hour of unscheduled time before speaking was a welcome benefit. I sat at the back of the conference room responding to emails that I'd received during my flight over. Eventually I heard the sound of chairs being pushed back in the dining room. I moved to my speaking position at the front of the room and waited for the arrival of 100 corporate CEOs. They never arrived.

It turned out that after the announcement that there would only be one after-lunch speaker, the conversation had turned to concerns about the increasing snowfall and access to the main arterial routes out of the area. So, one after another, the attendees had simply walked out of the venue and sped away in their late-model European cars.

I was left standing on stage looking at the organiser and host, three event staff members and a team of technicians. I had just spent 28 hours on a plane to talk to an empty room. Sometimes in saying yes, there were calamities or mishaps that I could only chalk up to learning. Life is like that. Even with the best of intentions, life sometimes delivers unexpected outcomes. Letting unexpected events form part of the make-up of who you are is much more empowering than seeing these events as failures.

When you talk to professionals in their thirties, the phase in their life beyond 50 feels like an eternity away. There is something lacklustre about the way that middle age is portrayed. The upper side of 50 is painted as unexceptional and predictable. This portrayal, by the media, in movies and by the economic systems we operate in, is unfair. I am discovering that there is so much to look forward to in the second half of my life, as I combine the joys of grown-up children, close-knit friends, rich life experiences and new knowledge. I no longer have to prove myself or justify my capabilities. However, I do know that I will increasingly be measured by my understanding of the new world – the technologies, new economic models and changing values.

Many of my female peers talk about becoming increasingly invisible as they age. These friends hold the common view that when they were in their thirties the extent of their expertise was questioned by their older counterparts – a lingering gender-based bias in business. For a brief period in their forties, their age was just right. They were old enough to be credible, but also young enough to be relevant. By the time they turned 50, they felt less accepted in some conversations, because they were seen to have less understanding of the new world compared with their younger colleagues. It's a bit like Goldilocks trying to find the perfect bed – in your thirties the bed is too soft and in your fifties the bed is too hard. For a fleeting moment in your forties there is the perfect moment, when you're young enough to be current and contemporary, and old enough to have the right level of experience.

I'm not surprised by age-based judgement, as it's constantly reinforced in media, politics, entertainment and sports. Certain capabilities are tied to specific ages from the moment we are born. Even as children, we are measured and judged on when we walk, talk, understand algebra or ride a bike. Standardisations and norms are reflected in all parts of life and few people challenge them. Subconsciously, we move to fit within these parameters of expectation. There is an unwritten rule for when we should start to do something new, from learning to skateboard to taking up a new field of study.

I feel so passionately about changing these perceptions that one of the standard scholarships I offer for the postgraduate studies in my institute is for students over 60 years of age. I love these students. They are committed, open and eager to understand new ideas. I appreciate this group is a subgroup of their contemporaries for their willingness to learn and undertake further study as a mature student, but I don't think they're that unique. I think this openness to learning is reflective of a large group of people aged over 60 who want to be valued and connected to the world around them. Sixty is the new 40. Well, at least that's my story and I'm planning to live by it.

Recently I crossed over the 50-year line – the year when I would stop saying yes to all requests. Now I have a new plan. My next 15 years will be my growth years. I'm committed to saying yes to anything that grows me as a person. While I may spend less time at the boardroom table or heading teams, I plan to spend more time learning, trying new experiences and discovering new passions. One of my greatest fears is facing the day when I am openly given leniency, or less accountability, because of my advancing age.

My days of flying across the world for short speaking engagements came to a stop a year before Covid-19. My regular airline had sent me a Christmas message showing the number of air miles I had accrued in the previous year. I was shocked to see my excessive carbon footprint and I realised the hypocrisy of my commitment to reducing my carbon footprint in other areas of my life. Covid-19 changed things up again. Now I speak at more international conferences than ever, but due to technological advances my audiences now sit within a screen. The line-up of small faces looking out of my laptop at me always reminds me of the beginning of *The Muppet Show*, when all the characters appear in small windows on the TV screen. I miss looking out at an audience and watching as attendees process new information. I hope there will soon be a technology that transitions online video to a rich, immersive online experience. We are all learning new ways to connect in a world where we work from our kitchen tables, our children's bedrooms and the cafe down the street. Engagement with our peers and our clients is changing. What comes next will be a step change in the way we work, live and communicate.

I am thankful for the opportunities my life has given me so far. There is still an abundance of living to be had, and endless new things to learn. I hope that by thinking about what matters to you and committing to a future that reflects the world you want to live in, you will make changes that empower you and enable you to thrive in whatever way your heart desires.

My future, your future and our children's future may be part of a global collective of nearly eight billion people, but we're also all unique individuals who have the ability to impact, enhance and embrace others. I hope you live your life with the freedom to be who you are without regrets. I chose to say yes to prevent me from saying no. We all need to identify self-limiting actions that stop us from living the life we dream. Every day is a new day, and I'm just getting started.